# the EDIBLE GARDEN

# HERBS

&

# FLOWERS

# *Rosalind Creasy*

Special Edition for the National Home Gardening Club®

THE EDIBLE GARDEN
Herbs & Flowers
Special Edition for the
National Home Gardening Club®

First published in 1999 by
Periplus Editions (HK) Ltd.,
with editorial offices at 153 Milk Street,
Boston, Massachusetts 02109 and
5 Little Road #08-01
Singapore 536983.

Library of Congress Cataloging-in-Publication Data

Creasy, Rosalind.
    The Edible Herb Garden / by Rosalind Creasy.—1st ed.
        p.  cm.
    Includes bibliographical references (p.  )
    ISBN 1-58159-077-6
    1. Cookery (Herbs). 2. Herbs. 3. Herb gardening. I. Title.
TX819.H4C7397 1999
641.6'57--dc21                              98-34729
                                            CIP
Creasy, Rosalind.
    The edible flower garden / by Rosalind Creasy.—1st ed.
        p.  cm.
    Includes bibliographical references (p.   ).
    1. Flower gardening. 2. Flowers. 3. Plants, Edible. 4. Cookery
(Flowers)     I. Title.
    SB405.C765  1999
    635.9—dc21                               98-36999
                                            CIP


First edition
05  04  03  02  01  00  99
10  9  8  7  6  5  4  3  2  1

Design by Kathryn Sky-Peck

Printed in USA

# Foreword

When I grew up, in my little world there were only two herbs: dill in pickles and sage in my Thanksgiving stuffing. My flower feasting was even more limited. In this case, it was only when I was visiting my grandmother when my cousin and I would occasionally sneak into a cranky neighbor's garden and filch a honeysuckle blossom or two.

Today, I can't roast potatoes without rosemary or make pizza without fresh basil and oregano; and a summer salad without nasturtium or chive petals looks naked to me. Further, growing herbs and many of the edible flowers is the most relaxing part of my garden experience. Unlike vegetables that may need to be covered with rowcovers to keep off the insects —or delphiniums that need staking —my chives, fennel, oregano, tarragon and thyme ask only to be cut back a few times a year. Caring for most edible flowers is not burdensome either. Once planted, my pansies, dianthus, borage and nasturtiums keep chugging along for months with only an occasional shot of fertilizer.

I hope you will find growing herbs and edible flowers as rewarding as I do. To help you along, I have shared with you many of my gardens, including their successes and failures, and assembled years of experiences from the many gardeners I have visited around the country. I learned, for instance, that Jim Wilson in North Carolina grows most of his herbs in containers because he has nematode problems; that Carole Saville has moved many of her herbs from New Jersey, to Los Angeles, and then to Berkeley and the great majority grow well in all these different climates; and that Cathy Barash had great success overwintering pineapple guava indoors in her Long Island home. I also know that most of you have trouble growing cilantro (see the reasons in the Encyclopedia) and have yet to discover savory (you'll be delighted). Armed with the information in this book, growing herbs and edible flowers will only add joy to your life.

— Rosalind Creasy

# contents

## PART I: CULINARY HERB GARDENS

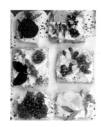

### Culinary Herb Gardens, *page* 1

*How To Grow an Herb Garden 6*
*Harvesting Your Herbs 12*
*Herb Garden Design 16*
*Herbs in Containers 26*

### Encyclopedia of Culinary Herbs, *page* 33

*From Angelica to Thyme*

### Favorite Herb Recipes, *page* 63

*Featuring Herbal Flavors 66*
*Fresh Herb Blends 66*
*Dry Herb Blends 68*
*Pestos 69*
*Herb Vinegars 70*
*Herb Oils 70*
*Herb Teas 71*
*Herb Butter and Cream 72*
*Interview: The Saville Herb Garden 74*
*Gudi's Potato Pancakes with Chives 78*
*Salmon, Cream Cheese, and Chive Torta 79*
*Fancy Carrot and Onion Soup 80*
*Watermelon Salad with Black Grapes and*
*  Tarragon 81*
*Goat Cheese Cheesecake with Herbs 81*
*Party Spinach Feta Strudel 82*
*Spinach and Fresh Oregano Pizza 83*
*Roast Lamb with Rosemary 84*

*Grilled Swordfish with Rosemary 84*
*Native Squash Stew 86*
*Barbecued Vegetables on Rosemary Skewers 86*
*Savory Mashed Potatoes with Garden Herbs 89*
*Stuffed Zucchini Blossoms with Goat Cheese 89*
*Fennel Rice with Pistachios 90*
*Leeks and New Potatoes with Savory Cream 91*
*Carrots and Apricots with Fresh Chervil 92*
*Golden Beets with Dill Vinaigrette 93*

# PART II: EDIBLE FLOWER GARDENS

## Edible Flower Gardens *page* 95

*How to Grow Edible Flowers 104*
*My Edible Flower Gardens 110*
*Interview: Alice Waters 120*

## Encyclopedia of Edible Flowers *page* 123

*From Anise Hyssop to Violets*

## Favorite Flower Recipes *page* 161

*Flower Butters 164*
*Sweet Things 165*
*Candied Flowers 166*
*Edible Flower Canapés 168*
*Tulip and Endive Appetizer 169*
*Citrus Dip for Begonia Blossoms 170*
*Pineapple Sage Salsa 170*
*Ricotta-Stuffed Zucchini Flowers 171*
*Sage Tempura 171*
*Flower Confetti Salad 172*
*Wild Violet Salad 173*
*Baby-Shower Petal Salad 174*
*Mardi Gras Salad with Pecans 175*
*Poor-Man's Pilaf 176*
*Stir-Fried Beef with Anise Hyssop 177*
*Rose Petal Syrup 178*
*Rose Petal Sorbet 179*
*Lavender Ice Cream 179*
*Tangelo and Kiwi Salad with Orange Blossoms 180*
*Scented Geranium, Crème Fraîche, and Strawberries 181*
*Tea Cake with Anise Hyssop and Lemon 182*
*Lavender Shortbreads 182*

## Appendices *page* 184

*Appendix A: Planting and Maintenance 184*
*Appendix B: Pest and Disease Control 192*
*Herb Resources 196*
*Flower Resources 198*
*Acknowledgments 201*

# culinary herb gardens

What a luxury it is to have a garden full of herbs! Even this country's best chefs usually can't match the meals created from such a garden. Imagine having enough lemon thyme or fennel to be able to use the prunings for smoking pheasant or salmon. Think of creating a salad, as if from the heart of France, with fresh tarragon and chervil, or making a Thai salad with real Thai basil. Fresh herbs are the signature of a chef and often a specific cuisine, yet very few markets in this country offer more than a meager selection.

When I think back on my cooking of years ago, it feels as though I was

This harvest of fresh herbs (*left*) is every chef's dream. Included are many of the stars of the culinary herb garden; (*clockwise from the top*) chives, French thyme, purple sage, sage flowers, silver lemon thyme, sage buds, rosemary, and French tarragon. In the middle are sprigs of Italian flat-leaf parsley and the flowers of German chamomile.

working in black and white and monaural. The form was there and it was enjoyable, but the depth and richness were missing. Now that I regularly use fresh herbs, I'm cooking in full color and stereo. The zip of fresh mint or the many flavors of thyme give the dishes more dimension. Twenty years ago I started on my herb adventure by adding fresh chives to potato soup and fresh basil to spaghetti sauce. What a difference! I went on to use fresh dill on fish, pesto on pasta, and herb vinegars on salads. Now, after years of

exposure to the full range of herbs, and thanks to many people's guidance, I use many more in my cooking, and almost all of them are fresh.

Herbs are the easiest to grow of all the edible plants and are great for beginning gardeners. Another incentive is that cooking with herbs can be a very healthful way to add excitement to meals. At a time when the safety of the salt and fats in our diet is being seriously questioned, it's a relief to explore enjoyable substitutes. I get so tired of being deprived in the effort to be "good." Using herbs deepens the pleasure as well as the healthfulness of food.

As I mentioned, my education in herb cookery started slowly. I was always an avid gardener, so years ago I put in a basil plant or two and some dill and chives, and that's still a good way to start. My serious interest in herbs took hold when I visited the herb garden at Caprilands in

Coventry, Connecticut. This extensive garden, fueled by the enthusiasm of the late Adelma Simmons, actually contains many different kinds of herb gardens: one that attracts butterflies, an all-gray one, a garden full of scented geraniums, and another with herbs for drying. At Caprilands, my sister and I enjoyed a meal in which herbs were used in each course, and Adelma came around while we ate to talk about which ones we were enjoying. That trip to Caprilands opened my eyes to the vast world of herbs and their many possibilities.

Since then I have visited many public herb gardens, and I highly recommend them to other interested gardeners and cooks. Visiting these gar-

dens is a great way to learn to identify the appearance, smell, and flavor of individual herbs. This country has hundreds of beautiful public herb gardens. Try a visit to our nation's herb garden in Washington, D.C., at the United States National Arboretum, or to the Cloisters, with its wonderful medieval garden, in New York City. Or sample herbs at the magnificent formal herb gardens at the Missouri and Chicago botanical gardens and the historical gardens at Old Sturbridge Village and Monticello. All grow a wonderful range of herbs and usually provide a guide to help you identify them.

Once I had a working knowledge of most of the herbs, I found I needed the help of creative cooks to explore

A small collection of herb containers (*below*) adorns my rose patio. The pineapple mint, sage, and lemon balm shown here grow well in all but the hottest humid climates.

There are dozens of varieties of thyme and I chose six different ones to set off my bird bath (*right*). In the perimeter beds I planted chives, scented geraniums, golden sage, and a selection of salad greens. To unify this little garden I included the showy, but decidedly not edible, tall graceful foxgloves and blue star creeper (*Laurentia fluviatilis*) in between the boards.

herbs in the kitchen. For every one way I thought of to use an herb, someone like herb maven Carole Saville or Rose Marie Nichols McGee (who was raised in the shadow of Nichols Garden Nursery, a well-known herb supplier) had created ten. And in the hands of master chefs such as the late Tom McCombie of Chez T.J.'s in Mountain View, California, and Ron Zimmerman of the Herbfarm outside Seattle, Washington, dishes came alive with herbs.

Both Carole Saville and Rose Marie McGee grew demonstration gardens for this book to put their creative information together and show us how simply and elegantly herb gardens can be created. In the process, they shared much information on how to maintain and cook from these gardens.

One final comment before we proceed. You might be totally unacquainted with some of the herbs covered here. In my research I was struck by how much of our available information and our emphasis on growing and cooking herbs comes from Europe. This is a wonderful bank of knowledge, but it excludes the many cultures around the world that season their foods with native plants. These so-called exotic herbs have a place in the new world cuisine, and I have included them here. I know you will find them as exciting as I have.

Golden sage, chives, French thyme, Spanish lavender, and rosemary in containers (*right*) greet visitors to my garden. In the beds curly parsley, winter savory, Oriental chives, oregano, and flowers line the walk.

# how to
# grow an
# herb garden

Jim Wilson, owner of Savory Farms wholesale herb growers, came to visit me one day, and as he walked up my herb-lined front path, he became completely engrossed in the plants before I could usher him into the house. He kept leaning down and rubbing his hands over the foliage. "Your thyme and tarragon grow so much more lushly than ours," he said. "We have problems with nematodes and wilt diseases." He was clearly envious of the 'Greek' oregano.  Jim, probably best known to most gardeners as the one-time Southern host of the *Victory Garden* television show, grows his herbs in humid South Carolina in a climate very different from that of dry California. As we renewed our old friendship, the subject of herbs came up again and again, and we compared notes about the different species and how they grew in the different parts of the country. How we see, say, lovage and angelica grow to seven feet tall in New York, yet only to three feet tall in Texas; how scented geraniums are perennial and five feet across in San Diego but grow as annuals only two feet tall in Idaho. Despite the differences, though, we were struck by how most gardeners can grow most herbs and how all can have a wonderful time doing it.

## Growing Herbs

The majority of herbs are perennial plants that need six to eight hours of sun daily, very well drained soil, little fertilizing, and spring pruning for renewal. In areas of the country where the ground freezes, most might need only mulching, although tender herbs such as rosemary and lemon verbena must be brought inside in the winter in cold climates. Alternatively, they can be treated as annuals and replanted every spring. In arid climates they need irrigation (drip irrigation is ideal) and should be washed down occasionally to prevent spider mites.

In hot, humid climates, where plants are bothered by nematodes, fungus diseases, and high heat, perennial herbs can be planted every year in a new area of the garden or in containers. New research indicates that marigolds planted among herbs helps repel nematodes from plants in the ground. Where garden soil is poorly drained, containers can be a solution. Madalene Hill and Gwen Barclay, authors of *Southern Herb Growing* who are based in Texas, have had much success avoiding many diseases and mitigating the extreme heat by growing their herbs in raised beds and by mulching the plants with small-diameter gravel, sometimes called chicken scratch. The gravel helps promote drainage and reflects summer heat, thereby keeping the soil fairly cool.

The annual herbs, such as basil, dill, chervil, and cilantro, are grown in a somewhat different manner, as they need annual planting and better soil than the perennials.

In most cases, there are solutions to most cultural problems that might arise with herbs, and even gardeners with no yard at all can grow a few herbs on a sunny windowsill.

Herb plants can be planted in a simple dooryard cluster, in a flower

The herbs—nepitella (*bottom left corner*) and chives (*center*)—grow in a border of edible flowers including nasturtiums, violas, calendulas, and arugula. All thrive in full sun and moist, organic soil.

mulching, planting, irrigation methods, fertilizing, and composting. Appendix B provides an overall look at beneficial insects and the basics of pest and disease control. Let's start with a prototype starter herb garden.

## Herb Garden Basics

Before you begin growing many herbs, it helps to know that the great majority of them fall into two major categories: perennials, herbs that live for more than two seasons, and annuals, those herbs that live only one season. When you begin, it also helps to choose herbs that are generally easy to grow. In most climates these are the sun-loving perennials: thyme, oregano, French tarragon, and chives. All originated in Europe and, with the exception of chives, are drought-tolerant and need little fertilizing unless grown in sandy soils. In hot, humid climates and mild desert regions French tarragon can't tolerate the heat, so you might want to try Mexican tarragon (*Tagetes lucida*) instead, which is also easily grown and may be available from local nurseries (or ordered from many of the sources listed in the back of the book). The popular perennial herbs can be purchased as small plants at most local nurseries from spring through early fall.

There are few gardeners who grow herbs and don't include basil. While still easily grown, basil needs annual planting every spring, rich soil, and some TLC.

Basil seeds are available from your local nursery, but most beginning gardeners find it easiest to grow basil

border, in containers, or in a traditional formal knot garden, so-called because the plants are laid out to form intricate patterns when viewed from above. As a rule, because they need similar growing conditions, annual herbs are at home in a bed of annual flowers and/or vegetables or clustered together. Perennial herbs grow best surrounded by other perennial flowers and herbs. For ease of maintenance, the informal cluster of perennial herbs is hard to beat. But, if a formal knot garden has always been your dream, be prepared to give continual care. The plants will need constant clipping to look their

best. Whatever your choice regarding garden design, the most important factor concerning your herb garden is how close it is to the house. All the herb authorities I know agree that the closer your herbs are to the kitchen door, the more you will use them in your cooking.

The following section describes a small herb garden and covers general herb-growing basics, from planting to maintenance, based on the experiences of Rose Marie Nichols McGee and Carole Saville. Their gardens are more complex and show how varied herb gardens can be. Many gardeners are interested in container herbs, so that information is covered in the next section. The nitty-gritty of growing herbs is covered in Appendixes A and B. Appendix A has information on planning an herb garden, bed preparation,

from young nursery transplants. (If you prefer to start your own seeds, see "Starting from Seeds" in Appendix A.) When selecting your basil plants, avoid those that look yellow or wilted or have started to flower. (Note: In some nurseries basil seedlings are sold a dozen plants or so to a small four-inch container. When you take it home, gently separate the young plants and plant them out. Failure to separate the plants will create a sorry clump of basil.)

For your first herb garden, I suggest planting one plant each of thyme, tarragon, and oregano, two chive plants, and three or four basil plants. If you're new to cooking with herbs, learning to

grow and becoming comfortable cooking with these tried-and-true herbs will be all you need to make a dramatic change in your cooking as well as your gardening.

### Planting Your Herb Garden

Gardeners in cold-winter areas will do best to plant in the spring or early summer; gardeners in mild climates will be able to plant all but basil through the fall. To plant your herbs, clear an area of the garden that gets at least six hours (eight is better) of midday sun and has great drainage. If you live in a cool-summer area, try to locate the garden near masonry to

give extra heat for the basil. In hot-summer areas herbs grow best with late-afternoon shade. An area four feet by six feet will be enough for the suggested herbs.

Remove rocks and any clods, rake the area smooth, and spread four or five inches of organic matter or compost over the soil. With a spading fork, work it into the top six inches. Place your herbs with the short ones—thyme

My front entry overflows with herbs. In the ground are the showy society garlic (the mauve flowers are used in salads), chives, savory, borage, and thyme. In containers are nutmeg geranium, and many different sages and thymes.

and chives—in the front, tarragon in the middle, and the taller oregano and basil in the back. Thyme and chives will spread to about a foot, the others up to two feet, so space them accordingly. Dig a hole about a foot across for each herb and sprinkle a few tablespoons of bonemeal or other form of phosphorus around the bottom of each hole and mix it in well. In the holes for the basil plants, add a few coffee cans full of manure or good compost, then add a source of nitrogen such as a few tablespoons of blood meal or fish meal. Mix the amendments into the bottom of the hole.

Gently nudge each herb seedling out of its container by putting your hand over the top of the container, turning it over, and tapping it to loosen the plant. If roots are collected in a mass around the outside of the root ball, gently pull them apart and spread them out. Put the plant in its hole, making sure the crown of the plant is level with the bed. Cover the seedling with soil and firm it in place so there will be no air pockets.

If you are putting in a drip watering system, this is the time to lay your ooze tubing around the plants and secure them. Make a small watering

basin around the plant and fill it with water. (Many gardeners find it helpful to put a label next to each type of plant so they can identify their herbs.) Water a final and critical time to make sure all the roots have received a soaking. Mulch the area with two or three inches of mulching material to cut down on weeding and watering. Watch for slugs and earwigs on the basil—a flashlight foray the night after a watering will usually reveal these critters. Pick them by hand and drop them in soapy water to kill them.

Keep the new plants moist for the first week or so. Slowly start letting the plants get a little drier between waterings. Use your judgment—if it's very hot or windy, or if the plants start to wilt, water more often. If weeds come through the mulch, pull them so they will not compete with the herbs for water and nutrients.

To prepare the soil (*top*), spread four inches of compost and two inches of manure over the soil and work it in with a spading fork. Dig a hole four times the size of the herb's root ball and work in ¼ cup each of blood meal and bonemeal. Plant the herb at the depth it was in the container (*middle*) and press down around the plant. Install drip irrigation and mulch (*bottom*) with two inches of compost.

## Maintaining Your Herb Garden

After a few months your herbs will be growing well, and a watering maintenance schedule will become established. In climates where rain is reliable, you will probably need to water only during a drought or in very hot weather. In arid climates a weekly routine is sufficient for all but the basil, which may need watering every four or five days.

Fertilize basil every six weeks or so with fish emulsion or fish meal according to the directions on the package. If you don't have a chance to harvest your basil, when it gets large and starts to flower you will need to prune it back by taking clippers and removing the top half of the shoots. This will encourage the plant to put out lush new leaves instead of setting seeds and declining. Unless the soil is sandy, the rest of the herbs seldom need fertilizer.

Prune all the perennial herbs using hedge or hand shears in late spring. Most herbs need to be cut back by at least half, though if the plants are not growing vigorously, remove only a third of the growth. Oregano and

thyme are only hardy to USDA Zone 5, or to minus 10 to minus 20 degrees; chives to USDA Zone 3, or to minus 50 to minus 40 degrees; tarragon to USDA Zone 4, or minus 30 to minus 20 degrees; and in cold climates, all will overwinter best with three or four inches of a straw or compost mulch layered over them in the fall after the ground has frozen. The mulch is not used to keep them warm but to ensure that they will not heave out of the ground when the soil freezes and thaws.

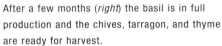

After a few months (*right*) the basil is in full production and the chives, tarragon, and thyme are ready for harvest.

Most common herbs and a few unusual ones (*right*) are available from local nurseries in small plastic containers. It's important to label your plants so you can identify them, especially those that are less common. In addition, I find I need to record the location and planting date of my new herbs in a journal because the labels sometimes get lost or become faded.

# harvesting your herbs

This basket (*right*) overflows with a harvest from my front herb border. It includes the unusual dittany of Crete (*Origanum dictamnus*), which is used in liqueurs, spilling out of the front, Mexican tarragon (*Tagetes lucida*), which is sometimes used in place of French tarragon, the mauve edible flowers of society garlic (*Tulbaghia violacea*), and bunches of rosemary, (*back left*), and oregano (*back right*).

For me, harvesting herbs often means a last-minute dash to the garden to pick a few leaves for cooking. When I have it together, though, I harvest a number of my favorite herbs and put them in a glass of water and place them on the windowsill above my sink. I then use them with abandon—all I need do is reach for a sprig or two. If I want to keep the herbs longer, I put them in the refrigerator, and they'll keep fresh for at least a week. To harvest larger amounts for preserving, choose a time when the herbs are at peak flavor, usually just before flowering, and when the plants are growing well enough to renew themselves. Another good time to harvest is when the plants need to be cut back to be renewed. Then one of the luxuries of having an herb garden is most evident, as you can use large amounts of the prunings for smoking. When you smoke fish or meat, place branches of green herbs such as thyme, lavender, fennel, rosemary, or dill over the wet wood chips before you close up the smoker. Voilà, lots of instant flavor.

## Harvesting the Seeds of Herbs

To harvest the seeds from dill, caraway, cumin, coriander, and fennel, start to assess their ripeness a few weeks after the plants bloom and when the seed heads start to turn brown. The seed heads of dill and fennel will shatter and shed their seeds more readily than the other herbs, and if you want to make sure to harvest all the seeds, tie a paper bag around the ripening seed head to catch the seeds. In all cases you can remove the seeds by hand once they have turned brown, or you can harvest the whole heads, leaving six inches of stem attached so you can tie the stems together. Dry the heads by hanging them upside down. First put a brown bag around the heads, secure it with a rubber band, and hang the bunches in a cool, dry place. When the heads are thoroughly dry, pull the seeds off the heads, put them in clean jars, and seal.

## Preserving Herbs

Fresh herbs are best in many cases, but most herbs are not available year-round, so good cooks over the years have learned ways to preserve the flavor. The best way to preserve an herb depends on the herb. As a rule, the dense, small-leafed herbs dry best, and the fleshy, larger leaves freeze well, either chopped or in butters. Most herbs are suitable for preserving in vinegar or oil.

## Drying Herbs

The following directions for drying herbs are best used for bay laurel, borage, chamomile, marjoram, mint, rosemary, sage, bay, chives, dill, lavender, lemon verbena, Mexican oregano, sweet woodruff, thyme, winter savory, and oregano.

Harvest all herbs in the driest part of the day and wash them if they're gritty, and pat them dry. There are different ways to pick and dry them. Some methods work best for herbs with large leaves, others for those with small leaves. You can easily pick the

single large leaves of sweet bay, lemon verbena, and borage and lay them out in a single layer on a screen; the long leaves of chives can be treated this way as well. I find it tedious to harvest herbs with small leaves and compact stems, such as thyme, rosemary, savory, chamomile, and sweet woodruff, as single leaves. I prune sprigs three or four inches long and lay them out on a screen; once the herbs are dry, the leaves can easily be stripped off the twigs. In all cases, for quick drying, you can put the screen with the leaves on it in an electric oven at a very low temperature (104°F) for a few hours; or in a gas stove just lay the herbs on cookie sheets, and the constant 95°F of the pilot light dries them in a day or so. If you have more time, place the screen in a warm, dry place indoors, such as a garage or attic, and dry for five to seven days. Stir the leaves once a day.

Herbs that grow fairly tall and produce long sprays, such as oregano, sage, mint, lavender, and lemon verbena, can be dried by hanging them in a warm, dry place. Create bunches bundled with a rubber band to hold the sprays together. (The rubber band will also hold them when they dry and shrink.) As I do this in my dusty garage, I like to cover the bundles with tissue paper to keep the herbs clean. Seed heads of dill, fennel, and caraway I handle in the same way, but I also put a paper bag over the heads so the seeds will not drop to the floor.

Some gardeners swear by drying herbs in the microwave oven. This works well for a small amount, but I

do find that the leaves get darker than when air-dried. Place cleaned herbs on a piece of paper towel and microwave them on high for a minute at a time. Rotate the herbs often. Repeat the process until the herbs are brittle dry. Dense herbs like rosemary will take longer than delicate ones like dill. When your herbs are dry, store them in airtight containers in a cool, dark place.

## Freezing Herbs

You can also preserve some herbs by freezing. I do this with fennel, dill, chervil, chives, tarragon, and mint. Just wash the herbs, pat them dry, and take the leaves off the stems. Leave them whole or chop them. Put the leaves in a self-sealing plastic freezer bag, press out the air, label, and freeze. You do not need to defrost them before using them in soups, sauces, and marinades. The herbs will have darkened and turned soft, but the flavor keeps for a good six months. Herbal butters are another way to freeze the flavor of herbs. (See the recipe on page 72.)

Garden sages (*left*) can spark the cook's imagination. Try making fritters with the flowering stalks, adding the leaves when you roast potatoes, and using the unusual foliage for garnishes.

# herb garden design

Pink, purple, and yellow flowers give warmth to my herb entry and help tie together the great variety of plants. The walk is lined with yellow species marigolds and gloriosa daisies, purple sage, and pink roses. The herbs include curly parsley, oregano, tricolor and golden sages, winter savory, anise hyssop, society garlic, and dittany of Crete.

As a landscape designer, I feel compelled to share with you a few of my own personal herb gardens and the design process I went through.

My favorite herb garden is the one I had installed in the front yard a few years ago. Instead of using the plants as the major feature, I used a strong geometric pattern formed by putting 2 x 12 boards in the ground in a ray pattern. For the focal point in the middle I placed a birdbath. I got the wood for free from the lumberyard since they had been cut off the end of larger boards that had been milled for other projects. (It took six months of visiting lumberyards, but it was worth it.) The boards were cut into long wedges and scored on the back with 1/8-inch-deep grooves to prevent them from cupping. They were then laid out in a ray pattern and secured in place by two layers of bender board nailed to both sides of the circle. I used all sorts of culinary herbs around the outside and toward the middle: thymes, oreganos, lavenders, tarragon, lemon balm, and chives, along with a few salad greens and disease-resistant roses. Within a year the ground cover had filled in and the plants looked mature enough to make it a magical garden. We still refer to it as the Magic Circle (see pages 24–25).

Another herb planting I enjoy is the herbal entry up my front steps and walk. In this case, while the steps and walk add design interest, it's the herbs and flowering plants that get the attention. I chose purple, yellow, and light pink as the color theme and filled in other parts of the garden with lots of variegated herbs. I think their white-and-green and white-and-gold leaves make a perfect foil for the deep hues of yellow and purple. I chose variegated lemon thyme, golden and tricolor sage, and golden oregano as the stars of the front border and added yellow violas in the spring and yellow species marigolds in the summer.

## The McGee Herb Garden

Rose Marie Nichols McGee grew up in Oregon next door to an herb nursery. Maybe I can be forgiven, therefore, when I say that she knows herbs from the ground up. For years I ordered herbs from her parents' company, Nichols Garden Nursery, and it seemed natural to contact them when I was searching for knowledgeable people to share information on herbs.

Rose Marie and her husband now own and manage the nursery, and she was very enthusiastic about growing a demonstration garden for me. She saw it as a great excuse to put in a small herb garden for her mother. Her mother has been hampered by arthritis for some years and missed having a garden. What a wonderful little garden the new one turned out to be! Rose Marie cut a modified kidney-shaped area, about ten by twenty feet in size, out of an existing lawn and filled it completely with herbs. The idea, she told me, was to make "an informal and inviting little oasis, with paths so my mother—or anyone!—could get right in and enjoy it."

The bed preparation was rather straightforward. Rose Marie began in late spring by digging up the area and then, to save a lot of weeding in the future, sifted through the soil to remove all the rhizomes of the weedy quack grass that had grown rampantly in the lawn. She then put on a layer of mushroom compost and hand tilled it in. Finally, to prevent another future problem and to give the garden a clean line, Rose Marie put in a black plastic edging to keep the lawn from growing into the herb bed.

One design objective was low maintenance, which meant making a perennial garden with spaces reserved for annual herbs like basil, calendulas, cilantro, dill, and nasturtiums. She explained: "This year, because it's new, I've added many annuals, but by next year the perennials will fill it in and be in their glory and I won't add many annuals. I enjoy having a constant supply of flowers and color in the garden for most of the season, so I chose many of the flowers to bloom at different times of the year."

Rose Marie decided to start the blooming season with sweet cicely, which blossoms in spring along with the daffodils and has white, lacy, very fragrant flowers. Other herbs that will bloom throughout the growing season include clary sage, which produces great spikes of lavender flowers; regular chives, with their lavender blossoms produced in late spring; Oriental chives, with white flowers that smell like roses and that bloom in July and August; two varieties of lavender that bloom most of the summer; lemon mint, which will

provide a lot of color in late August with its shaggy purple heads; and pineapple sage for late-fall color—its scarlet blossoms will brighten up the garden from September until it is cut down by frost and dies. During the first year annual plants yielded much of the garden's color—the purple foliage of 'Red Rubin' basil, orange and yellow nasturtiums and calendulas, and the large yellow heads of dill.

The garden was designed with low edging plants in the front and along

the paths, with a gradual increase in the height of the plants toward the middle and back. Rose Marie used as focal points for the design a dramatic angelica plant, with its large spreading leaves and handsome foliage, and two graceful statues of monks made by a local artist.

I asked Rose Marie to talk a bit about how she uses herbs from the garden. "I harvest angelica when it's just starting to bloom," she began, "because that's when it has the most flavor. I

don't let the flower heads develop at all. I then simply take the large stems and cut them up and boil them in a sugar syrup. Once they're candied and dried, I chop the stems and add them to my favorite shortbread recipe. Another herb I enjoy is sweet cicely. I use the foliage in salads during the year and the seeds in fruit or green salads. The seeds are tender and have a sweet anise flavor."

There was a great deal of basil in the garden, and I asked Rose Marie

how she prepared it. She told me that she and her mother preserve it by chopping the leaves and layering them in a jar alternately with layers of Parmesan cheese and then freezing it. They find that it keeps very well that way, and they sprinkle basil on vegetables and salads and use it in pesto and spaghetti sauce all winter long.

On my last day at Rose Marie's garden, she laid out a marvelous tea party—the very vision of a childhood fantasy, complete with scones with

scented basil jellies, shortbread with candied angelica, and lemon verbena tea. All the confections were wonderful, and all were filled with herbs!

## Designing Your Herb Garden

You can start herb gardening in numerous ways. For example, a few annual plants of basil, dill, chervil, and cilantro can be spotted around your vegetable garden or interplanted among flowers. In this case little soil preparation is needed beyond what you have done for the existing vegetables and flowers. Adding an occasional perennial herb like lavender, Oriental chives, sage, fennel, and thyme to a perennial flower border is easy too. Just loosen the soil and place the transplant in the soil, water it in and mulch the soil, water it again off and on for the first few weeks, and let the rains (or drip irrigation) and Mother Nature take over. If you are a beginning herb gardener and want to plant just a few herbs in a corner of your yard, then you might consult "Herb Garden Basics" on page 8. However, if you are planning a fairly extensive new herb garden, you will need to prepare the soil more carefully and design the beds for ease of access and for appearance.

The Nichols garden and the Saville garden (shown on page 75) are examples

Rose Marie Nichols McGee, of Nichols Garden Nursery, created this herb garden oasis in the middle of the back lawn of her mother's house. The garden includes sages, nasturtiums, thyme, lavenders, rosemary, and chives.

My magic circle herb garden is large, measuring forty feet by forty feet, and has room for many herbs and a few salad greens. It is a fairly formal design in that I used large plants to anchor the corners, created a geometric form in the middle, and placed similar colors and shapes of plants in repetitive patterns around the center. If I had wanted it to be more formal I would have used small clipped hedges to circle the birdbath and around the outside. Further, I would have repeated the same herbs in the perimeter beds.

maintain and has room for dozens of different herbs. For most designs, first lay out either strings or hoses along the ground to give you an idea of the area and a feel for the size and shape.

## Installing a Formal Herb Garden

If you want to install a traditional geometric herb garden, either of the two following simple and straightforward formal designs are an easy way to start. Mark off an area twenty feet by twenty feet. For the first design (see drawing, page 21, top), create bisecting paths that cut across the diagonal in an **X** and create four equal triangular beds. Another option is to choose bisecting paths that cross each other in the middle and form a cross, creating four squares (see page 21, bottom). To make both designs more interesting, place a square or round bed in the middle and put a focal point sundial, sculpture, or birdbath in the middle. Paths through any type of herb garden should be at least three feet across to give ample room to walk and use a wheelbarrow. Beds are generally limited to five feet across, as that is the average distance a person can reach into the bed to harvest or pull weeds from both sides. Consider putting a fence, wall, or hedge around the herb garden to give it a stronger design, and to keep out critters if need be.

Designers use many different techniques to create the feeling of formality. Here are a few tips for planning your own garden.

of two completely different layout styles that would work in any garden. The Nichols garden is an informal cluster of herbs in a free-form design located in the middle of a lawn. It is easy to install, and its informality requires little maintenance, as plants don't need to be continually pruned to be kept to a specific shape and size. The Saville garden, in contrast, is a more formal design and will take a few years for the hedges to become established. While certainly not high-maintenance, it will require more care

than the Nichols garden. Consider too my herb gardens—an entry garden with steps up the walk, a circular herb garden built around a birdbath, and a streetside herb border. Look too to the dozens of geometric traditional herb garden designs. Whether you choose an informal area on either side of your front walk, create an informal shape in the lawn, or install a formal herb garden off your patio, plan for an area not much more than 400 square feet. This is a good size for most gardeners and gardens. It is a manageable size to

• Create formal gardens using geometric shapes—not free-form lines.

• Use small hedges, traditionally boxwood, dwarf English lavender, or germander, to outline the beds and sometimes the perimeter.

• Clipped hedges and herbs or topiaries give a decidedly formal feeling to a garden.

• When you use the same plant many times (especially when you repeat them in the same location in all the geometric beds), it tightens the design and makes a garden feel more formal.

• Line paths of formal gardens with paving, gravel, or lawn grasses, not straw or compost.

• Formal gardens usually include a focal point or two to interest the eye. Place these in the middle of the garden, on the four corners, or in the middle of each geometric bed. Focal points can be plants in containers, birdbaths, statuary, or very showy plants such as tree roses or herbs with unusual foliage.

Bisecting paths (*above right*) cut across the sides of this formal herb garden. A round bed is cut out of the center and a focal point container is placed in the center. A small hedge borders the beds and yellow flowers are used at each inside corner to add interest. The second design (*bottom right*) is also geometric. Here a square bed is cut in the middle and given a fancy plant for a focal point. Repetitive plants have been used on the corners and the garden has been fenced to give it a sense of enclosure.

This lovely formal herb garden is at the Minneapolis Arboretum. Many cities have public herb gardens and they are a rewarding way to see how different herbs perform in your climate. The boxwood hedges, brick walk and edgings, and the geometric shapes of the beds give a sense of formality. Container plants are used as focal points. Here they contain rosemary and sweet bay, two plants that will not winter over in harsh winters, but that can be brought inside to a sun room or greenhouse. The arbors and trellises create outdoor rooms and give a feeling of enclosure to this garden. A similar effect can be used in the home garden to frame an herb garden, but the dimensions of the structures should be smaller and more in keeping with the intimacy of a home garden.

This informal Texas herb garden (*below, top*) belongs to Lucinda Hutson, author of many herb books. The terra-cotta statue gives it a regional identity, as does the informal bench in the background. Both act as focal points and unify the design. Rosemary, oregano, society garlic, and arugula that has gone to flower spill out of the beds with abandon.

I designed this hillside herb garden (*bottom*) with creeping thyme around the paving stones, and yarrows, rosemary, lavenders, and society garlic around the paths. More culinary herbs follow down the hill and include sages, fennel, and chives. The deer on the property have the consideration to leave them all alone.

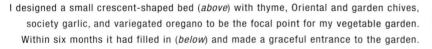

I designed a small crescent-shaped bed (*above*) with thyme, Oriental and garden chives, society garlic, and variegated oregano to be the focal point for my vegetable garden. Within six months it had filled in (*below*) and made a graceful entrance to the garden.

My magic circle herb garden (*right*) was made with eighteen, slightly tapered, three-foot-long wooden boards in a circle around a birdbath. I chose blue star creeper for the ground cover to fill in between the boards, and for color, nonedible foxgloves with their pink spires. It includes many varieties of thyme, chives, scented geraniums, cilantro, arugula, tarragon, lavenders, and sages.

# herbs in
# containers

Herbs make handsome container plants (*right*). They are compact, have a lovely range of foliage colors and textures, and most bloom at least once a year. Here the foliage of a purple sage contrasts with yellow and orange nasturtium flowers, and the spiky texture of the chives sets off the rounded nasturtium leaves.

I plant many herbs in my garden, but I've noticed that nowadays I'm growing an increasing number in containers—herbs on the patio are oh-so-handy to the kitchen, and, further, using herbs in containers gives me a range of design options. I liken it to hanging pictures in a room—spotting containers around my garden adds interest. If I feel like bright primary colors, I bring out my enamel containers; if I want a cottage-garden effect, I use my aged terra-cotta favorites.

Growing herbs in containers is also valuable for gardeners with small yards and for people forced to grow edibles in containers because their soil is infested with nematodes or root rots. In addition, as containers can be brought inside, in harsh-winter areas container growing may be the best way to grow tender perennials like rosemary and sweet marjoram.

## How to Grow Herbs in Containers

After years of trial and error, I've found five secrets for success with growing herbs in containers:

1. I use only soil mixes formulated for containers. I've found that garden soil drains poorly and pulls away from the sides of the container, allowing most of the water to run out, and it is often filled with weed seeds.

2. Since containers must have drainage holes in the bottom to prevent the plant from drowning, at planting time I cover the holes with a piece of window screening or small square of weed cloth to keep dirt in and slugs out.

(New evidence indicates that gravel or pottery shards in the bottom actually interfere with drainage.)

3. In hot weather, I now use only large containers, those large enough to provide generously for the plant's root system and hold enough soil so that the plant needs to be watered less often. I find that a small number of the small herbs like chives and thyme will grow in twelve-inch containers, but most grow best in large containers (eighteen inches or more in diameter). My Southern friends report that in their climate large containers are mandatory, as the roots on the south side of small pots bake in the hot sun.

4. After years of pale plants, I find I need to fertilize frequently and evenly. For me, biweekly doses of fish emulsion work well, as do granulated fish meal and slow-release fertilizer granules renewed every six weeks or so.

5. I find the most difficult aspect of container growing is to maintain the correct moisture in the soil. Succulent herbs like basil and chervil suffer when not watered enough; on the other hand, the Mediterranean drought-tolerant herbs succumb to root rot if given too much water, especially the sages. Once I learned how to water properly, I was on the road to success.

All gardeners need to learn to water container plants properly; even in rainy climates, hand-watering containers is usually a necessity, as little rain penetrates the umbrella of foliage covering a pot. I find that when I hand

water, it is most helpful to water the container twice. The first time pre-moistens the soil (I think of it as moistening a dry sponge), and the second watering is when I feel as though I am actually watering the soil. The opposite of underwatering is overwatering. To prevent this, I test the soil-moisture content with my finger before watering.

Watering container-grown herbs is critical for all gardeners, but it's of even greater importance for those of us who live in arid climates. After years of parched-looking plants, I finally installed a drip system. What a difference! I use Antelco's emitters, called "shrubblers" (available from plumbing-supply stores or by mail order from The Urban Farmer Store, 2833 Vincente Street, San Francisco, CA 94116), as they are tailored so each container on the system can have the exact amount of water it needs. My drip system is connected to an automatic timer, so it's scheduled to water every night for five minutes from spring through fall.

## Overwintering Herbs Indoors

As you can see, growing plants outside in containers has its challenges, and the problems are exacerbated when you bring the plants inside for the winter. In essence, you change a plant's

It's late spring in my garden and time to pot up young tarragon, lavender, and scented geraniums before the weather gets too hot and they need water twice a day. A harvest of curly parsley, to make a lovely cream soup, oregano for drying, and the purple flowers of the Mexican sage (*Salvia leucantha*) for a table bouquet, complete the scene.

Containers can become the focal point of a garden. Here an old wooden bucket filled with golden sage and a nail barrel with ornamentals and creeping rosemary draw the eye. In the background the flower spikes of anise hyssop attract bees, and in the foreground a winter savory peeks out from behind a species yellow marigold.

environment from a bright, sunny spot with fairly high humidity and a normal ecosystem and relocate it to a dim area with low humidity and no natural predators. It can be done, and done well, but it requires care, thought, the right plants, and a suitable sunny spot in the house. As a rule, herbs that tolerate shade are the most successful. If you plan to cook with many of the herbs, you will need more plants than usual, as herbs grown indoors over the winter grow more slowly than those outside.

1. Select a place in the house that gets at least six hours of direct sun a day. Temperatures in the sixty- to seventy-degree range and areas away from cold drafts are best. If a sunny window is not available, then set up an area with fluorescent lights. Locate fixtures six inches above the plants, and run them for sixteen hours a day.

2. Choose herbs that are fairly adaptable to indoor conditions, such as mint, parsley, winter savory, lemon balm, and scented geraniums. Chives grow fairly well indoors but tend to go dormant for part of the winter. If you have an attached greenhouse or bright sunroom, you might try the sun-loving bay, oregano, rosemary, sweet marjoram, and thyme as well.

3. For the best success, choose your

plants at the beginning of the growing season and plant them in containers from the outset instead of uprooting them in the fall. Containers at least eight inches across filled with commercial potting soil do best. These containers can be sunk in garden soil over the summer to keep watering to a minimum.

4. A few weeks before your first expected frost, prune back plants; check for aphids, scale, whiteflies, and mites; and treat if infested.

5. Place plants in a shady spot for a few weeks to acclimatize them to low light levels.

6. Just before bringing plants in, wash remaining foliage well and spray with a prophylactic dose of insecticidal soap.

7. Once they're inside, isolate outdoor plants from your houseplants until you have determined that neither is contaminated.

8. Water most overwintering plants only when the soil surface starts to dry out.

9. Wash down foliage occasionally to remove dust that can harbor spider mites.

10. Turn containers every week or so, so all sides receive equal light.

11. Fertilize monthly with half-strength fertilizer.

12. Maintain good air circulation and keep plants from touching, to prevent diseases and pests.

13. If your house is very dry, raise the humidity around your plants by filling a shallow tray with pebbles and placing it under your plants. Pour a half inch of water into the tray every few days.

Keep containers from sitting in the water, to avoid root rot.

14. Watch for pests; if they appear, immediately isolate any infested plants to prevent the problem from spreading, and treat them with insecticidal soap or send them to the compost pile.

Two large 'Tuscan Blue' rosemary trees and two sages, the purple 'Purpurascens' and a gray-leafed 'Extrakta,' in blue containers, adorn my front steps.

31

# encyclopedia of culinary herbs

The following is a detailed list of the most common culinary herbs. The basic cultural information about how to prepare the soil, planting techniques, seed starting, irrigation, mulching, fertilizing, pruning, and pest and disease control is covered in Appendixes A and B.

For each entry the common name of the herb is given as the title, followed by the herb's Latin name. The first word in a Latin name is the plant's genus, namely, a small group of plants that are closely related and similar to each other. The second name is the species. These are plants that are so closely related they are able to interbreed. When more than one species is being described in the

entry they are designated as *spp*. It is critical to use the Latin name of unfamiliar edible plants as the common names of plants change from region to region and may be used to describe plants that are not edible, even ones that are toxic.

The herbs I have chosen to cover here are my favorites. Many of the herb entries include named cultivated varieties that are designated by single quotes. These select varieties (also known as *cultivars*) are most often available only from specialty herb nurseries. I have chosen them for their unusual foliage or flavor variations and I find them worth seeking out.

I have also included a number of exotic herbs. Some have there own unique flavors, others have tastes similar to familiar herbs and can be used as substitutes for the more common herbs in the warmest summer areas. To purchase the more unusual varieties you need to seek out specialty herb growers.

Oregano and Roman chamomile work well in the mixed border that lines my front walk. On my way into the house I can harvest a few sprigs of oregano for my supper.

# ANGELICA
## *Angelica archangelica*

ANGELICA IS A LARGE-LEAFED herb that grows up to six feet and more. In humid climates it can be a dramatic backdrop to a flower border. Both the aromatic leaves and the stems impart a slight anise flavor and are used in numerous savory dishes.

**How to grow:** Angelica is a biennial that produces huge clusters of creamy yellow flowers in the summer, beginning in its second year. It's amazingly hardy, to USDA Zone 3, but it grows very poorly in the Deep South. It is started from seeds in rich, well-drained, slightly acidic soil. Keep it fairly moist during the growing season, and apply nitrogen if the foliage starts to yellow. Aphids and stem rot are occasional problems. In arid climates it grows less rampantly than in humid ones.

**How to prepare:** The fresh stems can be used sparingly to flavor salads. The stems can be preserved, most popularly by candying. To use the stems for candying, harvest them before they flower. The fresh leaves can also be used in salads and soups and cooked with fish or poultry. Angelica has been used to flavor liqueurs such as Chartreuse and vermouth for centuries.

Angelica

Anise

# ANISE
## *Pimpinella anisum*

SINCE ANCIENT TIMES anise has been enjoyed for its slightly licorice taste.

**How to grow:** Anise is an annual plant started from seed in the garden. Thin seedlings to six inches apart. The plants grow to about two feet and put out both lobed and feathery green leaves and umbels (flat flower heads that grow out from a central point) of cream-colored flowers. The ripe seeds are produced only in hot-summer areas. Anise is fussy about its growing conditions and needs full sun and moist, well-drained soil. Pick the seed heads when they start to mature, clean them, and store them in a warm, dry place.

**How to prepare:** The leaves can be used for seasoning soups or made into a tea, and the seeds are used in baked goods, including the traditional German *pfeffernuss* cookies, and sausages. Anise seeds can be used in place of caraway seeds in bread recipes. Anise is also used in liqueurs, salad dressings, and (my favorite way) spaghetti sauce and chicken cacciatore.

# ANISE HYSSOP

*Agastache foeniculum*

AN EXCEPTION IN THE HERB world, anise hyssop is native to the Western Hemisphere. Like artichokes, anise hyssop changes the chemical makeup of saliva, so subsequent foods tend to taste sweet.

**How to grow:** This highly ornamental plant is an easily grown herbaceous perennial that reaches from three to six feet and has gray-green leaves and striking, dense one- to three-inch flower spikes ranging from mauve to lavender to white. It is hardy to USDA Zone 4. Start anise hyssop from seeds or divisions and grow it in full sun in average soil, and keep it fairly moist. The plant dies down in the winter and often reseeds itself the next spring. It is bothered by few pests and diseases.

**How to prepare:** The young leaves and tiny petals of the sweet flowers have a flavor somewhat between anise and root beer; the leaves and petals, if used sparingly, are very pleasant in salads, iced drinks, soups, tea breads, and desserts. Great with mushrooms, this is one of the tastiest of the edible flowers.

Anise hyssop

# BASIL
## *Ocimum basilicum*

BASIL IS THE HERB most associated with Italy, yet it is native to Asia and Africa. It's a member of the mint family, and its aroma does in fact have "minty" overtones. There are different types of basil with familiar flavors, namely cinnamon, anise, and lemon, and different forms and foliage colors as well. (Someone calculated there were at least thirty varieties of basil available from specialty seed companies.)

**How to grow:** Basils are primarily annuals that glory in hot weather and will wither after a light frost. Gardeners in cool-summer areas struggle to keep basil going, as it needs many days in the eighties to grow well. Choose a well-drained area of the garden, in full sun or with a light amount of shade, where the soil is fairly fertile and has high amounts of organic matter. There are many basils to choose from. The familiar sweet basil is the most common and the most varied, as many purveyors have selected their own strains. You may want to buy sweet basil from different sources and see which ones you prefer. Variations include the large-leafed 'Lettuce-Leaf' and 'Genovese' and the even larger-leafed 'Mammoth' sweet basils. I urge you to try the lemon-, cinnamon-, and anise-flavored varieties too. 'Anise'

'African Blue,' 'Green Ruffles,' and 'Dark Opal' basil (*right*) grow in a bed with 'Tabasco' pepper at the National Herb Garden in Washington, D.C.

basil is a fairly large plant with purple-tinged foliage and has a strong anise-like aroma. 'Cinnamon' basil looks quite similar but has a perfumed cinnamon taste. The most dramatic basils, 'Red Rubin' and 'Purple Ruffles,' have deep purple foliage and pink flowers—great for coloring basil vinegar pink, but they make dreadful-looking brown pesto. 'Siam Queen' is a striking Thai basil with a spicy flavor and compact purple flower heads. There are a number of dwarf basils with small leaves that when planted in a row will neatly edge a flower or vegetable bed. They are 'Fino Verde,' 'Green Globe,' 'Green Bouquet,' 'Piccolo,' and 'Spicy Globe.' All taste great as well. Try also the lemon-flavored varieties, 'Sweet Dani' and 'Mrs. Burns' Famous Lemon Basil'—both are much more vigorous than the standard lemon basil. If your family loves basil, plan for four to six plants of sweet basil to give you enough for pesto, and one or two of a number of scented varieties for flavoring and coloring salads, marinades, vinegars, and oils. Basil plants can be grown in a vegetable garden but are at home in the flower border as well, combined with petunias, zinnias, and dwarf marigolds. The purple varieties and some of the colorful scented basils are stylish among peppers and bush beans.

You can start basil seeds inside to plant out later, and the more common varieties are also available as transplants in many nurseries in the spring or summer. Basil put out in the garden before the weather is really warm will just sit there and suffer. When starting seeds, be aware that basil seeds are

'Green Ruffles' basil

'Siam Queen' basil

Common basil

'Mrs. Burns' Famous Lemon Basil'

the plants with dolomite for a calcium deficiency.

You will be able to harvest leaves about eighty days from sowing and can usually continue until the first frost. Leaves may be picked or cut. If you don't keep the flower heads continually cut back, the plant will go to seed and give you few leaves. To further extend the season, bring in container-grown basil well before the first frost, or take sprigs off some of your garden plants and root them in water to keep them growing for a few months on a sunny windowsill. To keep your shoots vigorous, every so often add fertilizer to the water.

Basil is sometimes bothered by slugs and snails, as well as cucumber and Japanese beetles. Fusarium wilt is a growing problem; plants look healthy, and then either the whole plant or just a few branches start wilting and will not revive. Remove the plants and destroy them. Do not replant basil in the same soil for many consecutive years.

**How to prepare:** The aromatic leaves of basil are best used fresh in many dishes—soups, salads, stews, and spaghetti sauce, to name a few. To many people, basil is best known as the base for pesto, an Italian herb sauce. To others, it is the "only" accompaniment to fresh, ripe tomatoes. In France it flavors the famous *soupe au pistou,* a Provençal vegetable soup. Basil vinegars and oils add their rich perfume to salads all over the Mediterranean. Hindus float the seeds on top of sweet drinks for their reputed cooling effect.

slippery and are easily washed out of the row if you don't water them gently. They will sprout in about seven to ten days. Thin seedlings to about a foot apart. If starting your seeds inside, plant them a month before the weather warms up. Transplant them out into the garden, spacing them about a foot apart. Keep the plants fairly moist during the growing season. If your soil is not very fertile, feed them every six weeks, making sure they have enough nitrogen to keep the leaves quite green. If the leaves seem to pucker a lot (some is normal) and get small light yellow splotches, treat

# BAY LAUREL
(Sweet Bay, Grecian Laurel)
*Laurus nobilis*

THE AROMATIC LEAVES OF THE BAY tree have been used in cooking since Roman times. California bay (unrelated to sweet bay) is not considered culinary.

**How to grow:** Bay is a woody perennial. Purchase plants or grow them from seeds (you'll have a very long wait). Plant it in good, fast-draining soil. Bay laurel is not hardy, growing only to USDA Zone 8; in cold-winter areas plant it in containers and bring it inside to use as a houseplant. (Watch for scale insects, small shield-like casings attached to the bark, and treat with refined horticultural oil if they appear.) Harvest leaves as you need them. The leaves dry well and become sweeter when dried.

**How to prepare:** The strong, almost resinous-tasting leaves of bay are used in soups, stews, spaghetti sauces, and marinades. The flavor is better if the bay leaf is added toward the end of cooking. Be sure to remove bay leaves from dishes before you serve them.

# BORAGE
*Borago officinalis*

THIS HERB IS NATIVE to Europe and Africa and has a slight cucumber flavor.

**How to grow:** Borage is an easily grown summer annual that sometimes acts as a biennial. Borage plants grow to about two feet and have hairy gray leaves and deep blue, half-inch star-shaped flowers. The plants are easily started from seeds. Plant seeds in the spring in average soil and full sun after all threat of a frost is over. You can harvest young leaves once the plants are established, and flowers anytime they appear. Borage often reseeds itself.

**How to prepare:** Young leaves can be added to salads, and minced and added to soups. The one-inch borage flowers can be used in salads, to garnish soups, or to decorate desserts. They can also be crystallized. To make flowers edible, you must remove the hairy sepals from the flowers using the following simple procedure. With your left hand (if you are right-handed) grasp the stem of the flower. With your right hand gently pinch the middle of the star and pull. The flower (corolla) should separate from the sepals intact.

*Caution:* Pregnant and lactating women should avoid these as more than eight to ten flowers can cause milk to overflow!

Bay laurel

Borage

Caraway

Caraway

Salad burnet

# BURNET, SALAD

*Poterium sanguisorba*

THIS ATTRACTIVE PLANT produces leaves with a slight cucumber taste.

**How to grow:** Salad burnet is an easily grown perennial plant hardy to USDA Zone 3. Its green leaves look divided and mostly sprout from the crown. Start this lovely little plant from seeds or divisions in the spring. Plant it in full or partial sun in poor soil, keep it fairly moist, and cut off seed heads as they appear (or they will reseed in the garden). Burnet has few pests or diseases.

**How to prepare:** Harvest the young leaves and use them fresh in salads, as a garnish in summer drinks, and in sauces or vinegars. Burnet does not retain its flavor well when dried. For centuries Italians have gathered the young spring foliage of borage and salad burnet from the wild and added it to salads. Later in the season, when the leaves are more mature, they use them as a pot herb in combination with greens like spinach and chard in soups and risottos.

# CARAWAY

*Carum carvi*

THE PUNGENT SEEDS OF CARAWAY are a favorite seasoning in parts of northern Europe.

**How to grow:** Caraway is a biennial that produces carrotlike leaves the first year and flower heads and seeds the second year. It's hardy to USDA Zone 4. Sow the seeds in spring in a sunny, well-drained soil and keep them fairly moist. If the soil freezes in the winter, mulch the plants well. Harvest the seed heads a month after they have blossomed. Shake the heads into a paper bag and separate the seeds from the debris. Store them in a warm, dry place.

**How to prepare:** Caraway seeds give a distinctive flavor to many dishes. Add to vegetables, salads, rye breads, sauerkraut, and stuffed cabbage.

# CHAMOMILE

*Chamaemelum nobile;
Matricaria recutita*

THERE ARE TWO TYPES of chamomile: the perennial type, which is low-growing and moderately hardy, and an annual chamomile, which is a lovely short-lived garden flower.

**How to grow:** The annual chamomile, *matricaria recutita,* sometimes called German chamomile, grows to about eighteen inches and produces a cloud of small white daisies. It has a sweeter taste, is less medicinal, and is preferred by many for making tea over the perennial chamomile. Start both chamomiles from seed in well-prepared soil in full sun. Keep it fairly moist. Or plant perennial chamomile from plants available from the nursery. It is hardy to USDA Zone 4. Both are quite free of most pests and diseases.

**How to prepare:** Most cooks prefer the flavor of the annual chamomile. The perennial is most often used for medicinal purposes. Use the flower heads fresh or dried in herbal teas, and the petals in salads. The heads dry well for winter use.

German chamomile

Chervil

# CHERVIL

*Anthriscus cerefolium*

THIS DELICATE, LACY-LOOKING herb is used quite commonly in France. Its slightly anise flavor is a favorite in salads and sauces. Chervil is also one of the herbs that make up the traditional herbal mixture fines herbes.

**How to grow:** Chervil is an annual herb that grows best in cool weather; because it doesn't transplant well, it is generally sown in place in early spring and again in fall. Give the plants morning or filtered sun and rich soil, and keep them well watered. Chervil seeds need light to germinate. Plant seeds in shallow furrows a half inch deep and cover the furrows with damp cheesecloth. Keep the cheesecloth damp until the seeds germinate. Thin the seedlings to six inches to a foot apart. Begin to harvest sprigs when the plants are six inches tall. The plants are short-lived, so, as with

radishes and lettuces, to keep a supply, sow seeds every few weeks during the cool part of the spring and fall. In some climates if you allow the plants to go to seed, they reseed themselves.

**How to prepare:** Chervil wilts readily, so harvest it fresh as close to preparation time as possible. The delicate anise-flavored leaves of chervil are used fresh in salads, with eggs and salmon, in cream soups, in cream- and goat-cheese spreads, and chopped and added at the last minute to many classic sauces. It is hard to preserve the delicate flavor of chervil. Drying destroys its flavor; instead make a chervil butter and freeze it for up to two months.

# CHIVES

*Allium* spp.

CHIVES ARE ENJOYED by the herb sophisticate as well as the beginner, and they are so easy to grow that I sometimes refer to them as the herb with built-in training wheels. They also must be the easiest herb to cook with, as they enhance any dish suitable for onions.

**How to grow:** There are two types of culinary chives. *A. schoenoprasum,* sometimes called onion chives, has a mild onion flavor, tubular grasslike leaves from twelve to eighteen inches high, and globe-shaped lavender flowers. The second type of chives, *A. tuberosum,* Oriental or garlic chives, is a

Garlic, or Oriental chives

distant relative and has an onion/garlic flavor, flat leaves from eighteen inches to two feet tall, and white star-shaped flowers. Both are perennial plants hardy to USDA Zone 3. Onion chives are worldly plants native to most of the Northern Hemisphere; Oriental chives are native to Asia.

Both types of chives need at least six hours of sun a day, and average to rich, well-drained, moist soil. Chives are best planted in spring and can be obtained as divisions, purchased as transplants, or grown from seeds. *Richters Herb Catalogue* carries a few specialized varieties of onion chives, namely, 'Grolau,' bred for greenhouse and growing indoors, and 'Profusion,' a variety bred for its flowers, which remain edible for an extended time because they don't set seeds, a process that makes the flowers papery and inedible.

Plant onion chives in the front of, or as a border to, your herb or flower beds and in the vegetable garden. Oriental chives, as they are taller, look best interplanted among other herbs and flowers. Both types of chives grow well in containers. Plant them alone or combine them with other herbs such as thyme and parsley.

To keep chives growing well, apply nitrogen fertilizer in the spring or if leaves are yellow. In rainy areas supplemental watering is seldom needed, and pests (except for occasional aphids) and diseases are few and far between. Once your chive plants are a few months old, you can harvest them from spring through fall by cutting the leaves an inch above the crown of the plant.

Onion chives

Trim chives occasionally, as they can reseed and become a nuisance, especially the Oriental ones. Cut them back after flowering, and they will soon look new again. Divide your plants every three or four years to renew them.

**How to prepare:** Tasting as they do of onions, both types of chives are used whenever a mild onion flavor is needed in a salad, say, or in sauces, dips, and marinades. They can be substituted in recipes calling for scallions or be made into chive butter to melt over vegetables or combined with sour cream and cream or goat cheeses. Shower baked or mashed potatoes, creamy or clear soups, and omelets with chopped chives. The flower petals

of the onion chives are pleasantly crunchy when young, but fibrous and papery when mature. Pull apart the lavender florets and sprinkle them on your food as you would the leaves. Oriental chive leaves can be used chopped in stir-fries and dumplings and soups. There are special varieties available through Asian specialty seed companies. After blanching them, you can eat the resulting tender stalks and buds as you would a vegetable. Though not as tasty as fresh, both types of chives can be dried or frozen, either whole or chopped, or made into butters or preserved in vinegar.

# CILANTRO
(fresh coriander)
*Coriandrum sativum*

THIS PUNGENT HERB LOOKS something like parsley, but its taste is very different. It has an earthy flavor some people dislike strongly and others (like me) crave.

Known in the cooking of the Americas as cilantro, or even Chinese parsley, this herb is referred to as coriander in the Orient. Whether you call it cilantro or coriander, this herb is among the most popular in the world.

There are other herbs with this same seductive flavor, those Carole Saville calls cilantro mimics. They are culantro (*Eryngium foetidum*) and papaloquelite (*Porophyllum ruderale* subsp. *macro-cephalum*), both native to the Americas, and rau ram (*Polygonum odoratum*), also known as Vietnamese coriander. All grow best in warm weather, in the eighties, and can take little frost. Papaloquelite is an annual; the others are tender perennials. The first two can be started from seeds; rau ram is started from cuttings. The cilantro mimics are available from a few specialty herb nurseries.

Cilantro picked with the roots intact

**How to grow:** The standard cilantro is an easily grown annual herb that grows best in cool weather. It bolts to seed readily when the days start to lengthen and in warm weather. Therefore, it is best planted in the fall in all climates. In cold-winter areas the seeds will sprout the next spring after the ground thaws, and in mild-winter areas the plants will grow lush and tall.

(Cilantro tolerates light frosts.) In short-spring areas early plantings are more successful than later ones. One guaranteed way to grow under these conditions is to treat cilantro as a cut-and-come-again crop and plant seeds an inch apart and snip seedlings at ground level when they're three inches

tall; then replant every two weeks until the weather gets too warm.

Starting cilantro by seed is easy and more successful than transplanting. Plant seeds a quarter inch deep in rich, light soil and in full sun. Thin the seedlings to four to six inches apart. Keep the seedlings moist to ensure lush growth. The varieties most commonly available in nurseries, while adequate, are specifically grown for the world seed trade; their seeds are used as a spice called coriander. However, you can grow varieties selected for leaf production, such as 'Chinese,' 'Long Standing,' and 'Slo-Bolt,' available from numerous mail-order seed companies. Harvest the sprigs once plants are six inches tall. Fertilize the plants only if they get pale. Cilantro has few pests and diseases. When the roots are needed for a recipe, harvest whole, mature plants using a spading fork. First loosen the soil well around the roots so they won't break off in the ground. Cilantro flowers, tiny flat sprays of white petals, are also edible, as well as great for attracting beneficial insects to your garden.

**How to prepare:** Cilantro leaves are almost always used raw, as the flavor fades quickly when they are cooked. Generally they are chopped and sprinkled on a dish or mixed in after cooking to give it a distinct flavor. In many Asian and South American dishes cilantro is among the most important flavoring and the sometimes-recommended parsley is not a suitable substitute. There is no successful way to preserve the flavor of cilantro because it fades very quickly once the essential oils are exposed to the air.

Add the leaves sparingly to salads, guacamole, and stir-fries, fold them into cooked vegetable dishes and salsa, or use whole leaves as a garnish on Asian soups and in tacos, burritos, and quesadillas. The herbs most often used with cilantro are the many oreganos. Seasonings that complement cilantro are ginger, garlic, and cumin. The seeds of cilantro, called coriander seeds, can be harvested, dried, and used to season curries, cookies, and rice dishes. The seeds are most flavorful if they are toasted in a dry frying pan for a few minutes before you grind them with a mortar and pestle or in a spice grinder. Coriander (cilantro) roots are a favored seasoning in Southeast Asia, especially Thailand. They taste like a mellow cilantro. Plants grown under optimum cool temperatures in rich soil produce roots large enough to be satisfying. Chop the roots to use in stir-fries or to make a popular Thai green curry paste, and pound the roots with garlic and black pepper to use as a base to season numerous Thai dishes. In recipes that call for coriander root, you may substitute cilantro stems instead.

**Note:** Herbs such as dill, fennel, caraway, and cilantro (coriander) produce seeds that are added to cooked dishes. For the most flavor, before using these seeds toast them in a dry frying pan over low heat until they just begin to perfume the air. Toasting brings out the flavor of the seeds and adds a nuttiness to the final dish.

Cilantro

'Fernleaf' dill

'Rubrum' fennel

# DILL
## *Anethum graveolens*

DILL IS A EUROPEAN HERB famous in pickles, but it's also quite versatile and enjoyable in many different dishes. Both the young leaves and the seeds are used.

**How to grow:** Start these annual plants in the spring from seeds after the weather has warmed up. Plant them in full sun in well-drained, fertile soil. Make successive sowings for a continuous supply of fresh leaves. These ferny plants have flat sprays of yellow flowers and grow to three feet, so give them room to spread. Keep dill moist throughout the growing season and harvest the leaves as soon as the plants get four to five inches tall. Save the seed heads and dry them in a warm, dry place. The varieties 'Dukat' ('Tetra-dill'), 'Fernleaf,' and 'Bouquet' are shorter and more vigorous than the standard dill offered in nurseries.

**How to prepare:** Use dill leaves fresh in salads; omelets; vegetable dishes, especially with spinach, carrots, beets, and potatoes; and fish sauces and with mild soft cheeses. Use the seeds in pickling cucumbers, snap beans, carrots, and beets. Preserve the leaves of dill by drying them or putting them in vinegar or oil. Harvest the seeds, dry them, and keep them in a cool, dry place.

# FENNEL
## *Foeniculum vulgare*

THIS HERB HAS BEAUTIFUL, ferny foliage and a flavor reminiscent of licorice. It is favored in some cultures as a digestive.

**How to grow:** Though a perennial, fennel is usually grown as you would dill. Cut plants back in spring to keep the plant looking trim. A coppery-colored fennel variety called 'Rubrum' (bronze) is striking in the landscape. Keep the seed heads removed, as fennel will reseed and become a weed in many parts of the country. Fennel is a favorite food of the swallowtail butterfly larvae.

**How to prepare:** The leaves can be used in salads, sauces, soups, stews, omelets, and salad dressings, and on fish and pasta. Throw the dry plant prunings onto the barbecue when you are grilling fish for a great rich flavor. Use the seeds in spaghetti, soups, sauerkraut, and bread pudding. Preserve it as you would dill.

**Note:** Dill, fennel, chervil, parsley, and caraway are all members of the same botanical family, the *Apiaceae*. This family produces flat sprays of small flowers that are especially attractive to beneficial insects. As a bonus, the flowers are also edible and can be broken into small florets and added to salads or used as a garnish.

# LAVENDER
(English, aka French)
*Lavandula angustifolia (officinalis)*

THE SCENT OF LAVENDER is among the most treasured scents in the Western world. Few folks think of feasting with it, and so many miss the opportunity to enjoy it to a fuller extent.

**How to grow:** Lavender plants grow to a height of two to three feet and are hardy to USDA Zone 5. The foliage of most lavenders is gray and the flowers are lavender. Start lavender from cuttings or transplants and plant them in full sun. One variety 'Lavender Lady,' readily starts from seeds and, unlike most lavenders, will bloom the first year. Watering is usually needed only in arid climates and when the plant is grown in containers, and then only when the soil is fairly dry. Shear the plants back after they bloom. Like most of the Mediterranean herbs, lavender does poorly in heavy or poorly drained soil and will succumb to root rot readily. In hot weather, lavenders occasionally become infested with spider mites.

**How to prepare:** With the strong lemon-perfume taste of the petals of its two-inch flower heads, lavender is one of the most useful culinary flowers. Leaves and flower heads can be steeped for use in drinks, jellies, soufflés, sorbets, and ice cream. Use the petals sparingly in salads and soups, and as a garnish.

Lavender buds are one of the ingredients in the herb blend known as *herbes de Provence.*

English lavender

Lemongrass

# LEMONGRASS
## *Cymbopogon citratus*

AN AROMATIC GRASS-FAMILY herb with a rich lemon flavor, lemongrass is much prized in Southeast Asia.

**How to grow:** Native to the tropics, lemongrass can be grown outdoors in very mild climates and in containers in cold ones, and then brought inside for the winter. It's hardy into the mid-twenties. Purchase divisions from local nurseries and some specialty seed companies. (Sometimes stalks from the grocery store will root.) Plant the divisions in good, well-draining soil, in part shade. Fertilize the plants a few times during the growing season and keep the soil moist. Lemongrass has few disease and pest problems.

**How to prepare:** Harvest the white leafstalks at the base of the lemongrass plant once it's established and use it as a seasoning in Thai dishes; sparingly in light soups; in marinades and fish and chicken dishes; and as a wonderful refreshing tea. Mash the stalk before use, to release the oils when putting it in a soup, and mince it very fine if you're using lemongrass in a salad or stir-fry. When you use it whole, remove the lemongrass stalk from the dish before serving.

To preserve lemongrass, either dry it or freeze the fleshy stalks.

# LEMON VERBENA
## *Aloysia triphylla*

LEMON VERBENA is another tropical herb with a strong lemon flavor.

**How to grow:** Lemon verbena is a woody perennial shrub that grows to ten feet in mild-winter areas and is hardy to about 10°F. In most areas it will lose its leaves in winter. In cold-winter areas it can be grown well in containers and brought inside or grown in a greenhouse. Plants brought inside will lose their leaves and should be kept in a fairly cool place. Cut the plant back and repot it in early spring.

Purchase plants or start them from seeds. Starting from seeds is a slow process, however. In mild climates situ-

Lemon verbena and purple echinacea

48

ate plants in a sunny area of the garden in good soil. Lemon verbena produces sprays of tiny white flowers in summer. Prune it often to keep the plant looking trim. Once plants are a foot or so tall, harvest the leaves throughout the growing season.

**How to prepare:** Use the lemon flavor of this herb in fruit salads, jellies, and fruit drinks, as a tea or garnish, and with chicken or fish. The leaves dry well and retain their flavor.

Lemongrass and lemon verbena both contain the same primary chemical, citral, that gives them their "citrusy" flavor. The herbs can be used interchangeably in recipes, but both plants contain other flavorful chemicals as well, so the flavor of the final dish will have a subtle difference.

Lovage

# LOVAGE
*Levisticum officinale*

THIS LARGE EUROPEAN HERB has a strong flavor reminiscent of celery.

**How to grow:** Lovage is a perennial hardy to USDA Zone 3, but it is usually treated as an annual in hot, humid climates. Start seeds in the garden in late summer or fall. In the coldest areas start it inside and plant it out once the weather warms in spring. Plant lovage in full sun or partial shade in moist soil with good drainage. In moist areas the plant can grow to six feet, so give it lots of room and keep seed heads cut off, or the plant will reseed itself. Harvest young leaves once the plants are a foot high. Collect seed heads and dry them in a cool, dry place.

**How to prepare:** Use the young leaves sparingly in salads, soups, and stews, or with meat and poultry dishes. Chopped young stems can be used as you would celery. The stems can be candied, like angelica, frozen for winter use, or used in a *bouquet garni*. The seeds can be used to flavor pickles, soups, and baked goods.

# MINT
## *Mentha* spp.

MINTS HAVE THAT FAMILIAR clean and clear taste. The Egyptians, Greeks, Romans, and other cultures throughout Europe and Asia have used mint to flavor foods for eons.

How to grow: Mints are perennial plants, and most are hardy to USDA Zone 5, grow to two feet tall, have shiny green leaves, and are quite rangy. If not controlled, most can become invasive. Mints spread by underground runners, so they are best planted in containers or within rings of metal flashing in the ground to contain the roots. There are many different kinds of mint. Among the most commonly used culinary ones are spearmint, peppermint, apple mint, and pineapple mint. Rewarding for gardeners and cooks are the unusual, but easily grown, 'Grapefruit' mint, 'Orange' mint, 'Pineapple' mint, 'Mint the Best,' 'Curly' mint, 'Chocolate' mint, 'Lavender' mint, 'Persian' mint, and the very close relative lemon balm.

Nepitella, *Calamintha nepeta*, is another mint relative. There are other plants referred to as nepitella but calamint is the one most commonly available. It has a mint flavor with overtones of apple and thyme. The plant has small green leaves and pink or white flowers on small spikes. In Italy nepitella is used with mushrooms, eggplant, and in potato dishes. *Caution:* evidence indicates that nepitella should be avoided by pregnant woman.

Most mints prefer moist, sunny to partly sunny conditions. Set out the

**Spearmint and lemon balm**

plants in the spring; once they are growing vigorously, they can be harvested anytime throughout the year. Prune heavily two or three times a year to keep plants under control. Under some conditions mints are prone to whitefly infestation. Cut the plant back and spray with a soap-based pesticide. Rust is another problem that can infest mint. If you have a serious infestation of either, pull the plant out and start with new plants somewhere else in the garden. Mints bloom in midsummer. The flowers in some varieties are white; in others, lavender to violet. Cut off the seed heads of lemon balm, or it can seed itself and be a nuisance.

**How to prepare:** All the mints have a characteristic clean "minty" flavor. In addition, lemon balm has a citrus taste. The leaves are best used fresh, though they can be preserved by freezing and drying. Use them in cool drinks, in green salads, in Middle Eastern dishes such as tabouli, with cucumbers, in soups, and in savory sauces, particularly with mustard or garlic served with lamb. Popular in Southeast Asia, mints are used in salads, curries, and soups. Also try mint in sweet dishes—desserts, jellies, sauces, fruit salads, and, of course, with chocolate.

# OREGANO AND MARJORAM
## various spp.

WHEN YOU THINK OF OREGANO, think of its flavor, not the plant. There are a number of unrelated plants that have the essential oil—carvacrol—that gives all oregano-type plants the characteristic taste cooks favor. One of the most flavorful European oreganos is 'Greek' oregano, *Origanum vulgare* subspecies *hirtum*, a native to the Mediterranean, though sometimes this herb is used interchangeably with its close relative, Italian oregano, *O. x majoricum*. However, in much of South America and the Caribbean the term *oregano* usually refers to different and unrelated plants. *Plectranthus amboinicus*, Cuban oregano, and *Lippia graveolens* and *Poliomentha longiflora*, two Mexican oreganos, also smell and taste like oregano. To further confuse the oregano issue, the identification of good culinary European oreganos is difficult because of mislabeled and misidentified plants in nurseries. As Carole Saville says, "The key to the puzzle is your palate. If you find a plant at the nursery simply labeled 'oregano,' be suspicious." Taste it and see if it has a pleasant, spicy flavor before you purchase it. Herb mavens usually look for plants labeled 'Greek' oregano (*O. v.* subspecies *hirtum*, synonym *O. v. heracleoticum*) to find the best flavor. Sweet marjoram is another puzzle, as plants sold as sweet marjoram sometimes are really Italian oregano. Again, taste a leaf. Real sweet marjoram has a savory, sweet, pungent aroma and a taste of new-mown hay. If it is in bloom, you will notice that the buds look like little knots, hence the common name knotted marjoram.

**How to grow:** The European oreganos are rangy perennials native to the arid mountainsides of the eastern Mediterranean. Common and 'Greek' oregano are hardy to USDA Zone 5, but sweet marjoram can't withstand hard frosts and is often grown as a

Mexican oregano (*Poliomentha longiflora*)

'Greek' oregano

and has large, fleshy green leaves. The variegated form has white margins. The two Mexican oreganos are hardy only to USDA Zone 9, and both are fairly tall woody plants with a rangy growth habit.

**How to prepare:** The European oreganos are most commonly associated with a number of Italian sauces used with pizza, spaghetti, and marinades. They can also be used in soups, stews, salads, and most meat dishes. Unlike many herbs, European oreganos and sweet marjoram may be enjoyed both fresh and dried. I use them fresh when I want a mild, clean taste, and dry when I want a little more bite and an intense flavor. For

traditional uses of the Mexican oreganos, add the dried leaves to chili dishes and salsa; to fillings for burritos, tamales, and chiles rellenos; and as seasoning in such seafood dishes as stuffed fish and ceviche, and meat dishes such as pork stew and tripe soup. In some parts of Mexico the leaves are toasted before use. All oreganos but the Cuban oregano can be air-dried by hanging the cuttings in a warm, dry place or dried in a dehydrator or the microwave oven. They may also be preserved in vinegar.

summer annual. All must be planted in full sun in a light, fast-draining soil. To ensure the best flavor, start plants from transplants, cuttings, or divisions, not seeds. Cut plants back in late spring to encourage new growth and once again in midsummer to prevent them from becoming woody. Except in very sandy soils or in containers, moderate watering and little or no fertilizing will keep plants healthy. Root rots are a common problem in clay soils and in containers. Spider mites are occasional problems in hot weather and when plants are grown inside. Oreganos do poorly under hot, humid conditions and are treated as summer annuals in areas where the temperatures are regularly in the high eighties and above. Here, Cuban oregano, while very frost-sensitive, basks in the heat and humidity of summer. This handsome plant is related to coleus, grows to two feet tall,

Sweet marjoram

# PARSLEY

*Petroselinum crispum*

PARSLEY IS A VERSATILE and nutritious herb whose leaves are used in most of the world's cuisines in one form or another. There are two major types—the curly one is best for garnishing, and the tall, flat-leafed type often called Italian parsley is used primarily for cooking because of its deep flavor and sweetness.

**How to grow:** Parsleys are biennials generally treated as annuals. The curly types have dark green, curly, finely divided leaves and are neat and tidy-looking in the garden. They seldom grow more than a foot tall and are useful to form borders, to use in the front of herb and flower gardens, and they combine well with flowering plants in containers. Varieties include 'Frisca Curly,' 'Extra Curled Dwarf,' 'Green River,' 'Triplecurled,' 'Mosscurled,' and 'Krausa.' Flat-leaf or Italian parsley grows to two feet tall and is a somewhat rangy plant suitable for the middle of the herb border or in a vegetable garden. It's the preferred culinary parsley for flavoring many European dishes. Varieties include 'Gigante d' Italia' ('Giant Italian'), 'Catalogno,' and 'Single-Leaf' parsley. Standard curly parsley is used for flavoring and as a garnish.

Start seeds in the spring or buy plants from nurseries to set out. The plants do best in full sun and in rich, organic soil high in organic matter. Gardeners in the Deep South or in the western parts of USDA Zones 9 and 10 will have more success with parsley as a fall and winter plant. Parsley seeds take from two weeks up to a month to germinate. They will germinate more quickly if soaked in water for a few hours or if frozen in ice cubes for a few days. Don't let the seed bed dry out. Fertilize parsley midseason with nitrogen. Parsley will develop root rot problems in heavy or soggy soil, and it is the favored food for swallowtail butterfly larvae.

The flavor of parsley fades when the herb is dried. Some gardeners in cold climates grow parsley in a sunny window over the winter.

**How to prepare:** Harvest the outer leaves of parsley during the growing season. They are best used fresh, though they will retain some of their flavor when frozen or made into a butter. All parsleys are high in iron and vitamin C. This herb's refreshing, peppery flavor is compatible with most herbs. And to add complexity of flavor as well as to sneak in extra nutrition, I always add it to marinaras and meat sauces and seldom make a soup, casserole, or stew without it. Parsley can stand alone when its leaves are chopped up and served with new potatoes or added to tabouli, the Middle Eastern salad.

Flat-leaf parsley is one of the most popular herbs in Italy. *Soffrito* is a traditional base for soups, stews, and pasta sauces made from onions, celery, carrots, and lots of flat-leaf parsley sautéed in a little olive oil.

Curly parsley

Flat-leaf, or Italian parsley

# ROSEMARY
## *Rosmarinus officinalis*

ROSEMARY IS A PUNGENT, RESINOUS
herb native to the Mediterranean. Over
the years it has become one of my
favorite herbs, and at any one time I
must have four or five different types
growing in my garden.

**How to grow:** Rosemary is a
tender perennial grown from cuttings,
divisions, and occasionally from seed.
It needs full sun and fast-draining soil.
In mild, arid climates it is so lovely,
reliable, and versatile that it is used as a
landscaping plant. Prostrate varieties
spill over retaining walls and down
hillsides; upright ones are used as
trimmed or informal hedges and in
mixed, drought-tolerant borders. In
areas USDA Zone 8 and colder, it is
usually grown as an annual or enjoyed
in containers and brought inside for
the winter. Most varieties of rosemary

'Prostratus' and 'Arp' rosemary

produce a profusion of light blue flowers in the spring and then a sprinkling
of flowers throughout the summer.
The form of the plant can vary from
strongly upright to completely prostrate. The standard culinary rosemary

has the light blue flowers. 'Arp' rosemary is reputed to be the hardiest rosemary, hardy to 10°F; 'Miss Jessup's
Upright' and 'Tuscan Blue' have
unusually straight, woody stems, perfect for using as a flavorful skewer for
barbecued meats and vegetables.
'Irene' and 'Tuscan Blue' have dark
blue flowers, and 'Majorca Pink' has
pink ones. 'Prostratus' is compact and
trailing, great for containers and to
grow over retaining walls. You can
purchase many of the unusual varieties
from specialty herb nurseries, both
retail and mail-order. Gardeners everywhere will have trouble with root rot if
the soil drainage is poor, and spider
mites are occasional problems when
the weather is hot or the plants are
grown inside. Gardeners in the South
may have problems with nematodes
and may be forced to grow rosemary in
containers.

'Tuscan Blue' rosemary

**How to prepare:** The leaves can be harvested anytime during the growing season, though they will be most flavorful just before flowering. The flowers are edible and make a lovely confetti to sprinkle over salads and vegetable dishes. Preserve rosemary by drying or preserving it in vinegar or oil (see page 70). Rosemary lends its pinelike flavor to many dishes containing pork, veal, and lamb and is a favorite herb to add to soups, stews, breads or biscuits, and pizza toppings. Try it in marinades with garlic for grilling eggplant and mushrooms, or roast potatoes in the oven with olive oil, garlic, and rosemary. Use this herb sparingly, as the flavor is very strong.

# SAFFRON
*Crocus sativus*

PROBABLY ONE OF THE WORLD'S most expensive flavorings, saffron is the dried, pulverized stigmas of a fall-blooming crocus.

**How to grow:** Plant the corms of these crocuses in late summer. They are available from a few specialty seed companies and nurseries. Hardy to USDA Zone 6, these plants prefer rich, well-drained soil with some afternoon shade. Plant these pretty, mauve to purple crocuses in large quantities if you wish to harvest them for the saffron, because you'll need a lot of plants to yield a sufficient harvest. Divide and

replant every two years. *Caution:* Do not confuse this crocus with the autumn crocus, *Colchicum,* which is poisonous.

**How to prepare:** Remove the orange stigmas with tweezers, dry them for a few days, and store them in a covered jar in a warm, dry place. Grind and use them in rice dishes, including paella, with seafoods, and in East Indian dishes.

Saffron

'Berggarten' sage

# SAGE
*Salvia officinalis*

SAGE IS A POPULAR, PUNGENT herb best known for its use in the stuffing for Thanksgiving turkey, but it is also great with potatoes or sausages and in stews.

**How to grow:** Most culinary sages are perennials that can be grown from cuttings or seeds. Common sage and most of its cultivars are hardy to USDA Zone 4 if given protection in the coldest regions. The purple, tricolor, and pineapple sages are hardy only to USDA Zone 7. Most sages do poorly in hot, humid climates and are treated as annuals in the Deep South. Plant sages in average soil, in full sun, and in soil with extremely good drainage. Sages die readily in heavy clay or if their roots stay damp. In hot weather, and with house-grown sages, spider mites are an occasional problem. Plants range in height from two to four feet. Numerous sages can be used in landscaping situations, in traditional herb gardens, and in containers. Most have gray foliage and purple flowers, but some have variegated foliage in colors of yellow, green, pink, and white. To keep these plants looking neat, trim them back once heavily in spring and, if they are leggy, again in summer. Garden sage is the most commonly used culinary variety. It has gray-green leaves and lavender flowers. 'Berggarten' is a robust sage with striking, large, oval gray leaves. Golden sage, 'Icterina,' while colorful in the garden, is somewhat less preferred in the kitchen and does not bloom. Purple sage, 'Purpurascens,' has soft, aromatic purple leaves and purple flowers. Pineapple sage, *S. elegans*, which is propagated only by cuttings or

Garden sage

divisions, grows to four feet tall and produces spikes of bright red flowers that are loved by hummingbirds.

**How to prepare:** The leaves of common garden sage are a favorite seasoning for all types of poultry, stuffings, sausages, and fish, as well as in soup, stews, cheeses, saltimbocca, and tomato sauces. Try adding sage when you roast potatoes. A famous Italian dish is baked white beans with garlic and sage. The flowers of all the sages that bloom are edible and can be sprinkled over salads, and the spikes of common sage are great dipped in a tempura batter and deep-fried. The leaves of pineapple sage have a distinctive pineapple taste and are used for teas and cold drinks and in fruit salads, jams, jellies, and salsas. The flowers can be used in fruit salads too and as garnish for pastries. Dried, the leaves of garden sage retain their flavor well, but the oils tend to get rancid, so for long storage, refrigerate or freeze.

Three sages: 'Berggarten,' 'Icterina,' and 'Tricolor'

# SAVORY

*Satureja* spp.

SUMMER AND WINTER SAVORIES are favored herbs from the Mediterranean. The most popular savory for culinary purposes is summer savory, called the bean herb in Germany.

**How to grow:** Summer savory is an easily grown annual plant that reaches eighteen inches in height. It has very small gray-green leaves and small lavender to white flowers that bloom all summer long. Use the plants in a flower border, in containers, or in an herb garden. Start seeds in spring $^{1}/_{8}$ inch deep in good soil in a sunny area. Keep both the seed bed and the ensuing plants moist. Harvest the herb once the plants are six inches tall.

Winter savory is a perennial that grows from six to eighteen inches tall. It has compact, bright green foliage and tiny spikes of white flowers, and it makes a handsome plant in the garden. There is a graceful creeping savory, *S. repandra,* that spills out of containers and can be used as a small-area ground cover. Winter savory, while slow to germinate, can be started from seeds, but it is usually propagated by cuttings or division. It is hardy to USDA Zone 6 and grows slowly. Plant it in full sun in sandy soil, and keep the plants somewhat moist during the growing season. Prune it in spring and again midsummer in mild climates, to keep it from becoming woody.

**How to prepare:** Summer savory can be harvested throughout the summer and is best used fresh. Winter savory can be harvested throughout the season and is somewhat more successful preserved for winter use by freezing or drying. Better yet, keep the plant in a container and bring it inside for the winter. Savory adds a richness to foods. I like to use it in small amounts when I use other herbs like oregano, thyme, or parsley and in onion dishes. Add a pinch when you sauté or steam carrots or potatoes. Use savories in salads, soups, sauces, and stews and with poultry. And once you've tried putting a few sprigs of savory in your beans, whether they be French filet (young string beans) or pintos, you'll never fix them naked again.

Winter savory

Summer savory

# SORREL

*Rumex acetosa,*
*R. scutatus*

SORREL IS A SLIGHTLY LEMON-
flavored green herb that is sometimes
cooked as a vegetable.

**How to grow:** There are two types
of sorrel. Garden sorrel, *Rumex acetosa,*
often mistakenly called French sorrel,
and the true French sorrel, *R. scutatus,*
sometimes called buckler sorrel.
Garden sorrel is a fairly coarse-looking
plant that grows to two feet tall with
six-inch-long sword-shaped leaves.
True French sorrel is a much smaller
and refined plant, growing only to six
inches tall with leaves an inch or so
across. Both are very hardy plants, to
USDA Zone 3, and flourish in all but
the most extreme climates. Sorrels are
generally planted from divisions,
though they can also be planted from
seeds in the spring. Locate plants in full
sun or with some afternoon shade in
rich, well-drained soil that is kept fairly
moist. As sorrels can sometimes spread
and become weeds, put them in the
garden where they can be contained by
paths or retaining walls, or grow them
in containers. Fertilize in the spring
and again in summer if the plants look
pale. Divide the plants every three
years to renew them. Protect the plants
from slugs and snails, which relish the
tender leaves.

Garden sorrel (*top*); and true French sorrel, (*below*)

**How to prepare:** Sorrel leaves
are used fresh in salads and sauces,
particularly those for fish and asparagus. Try this herb in a savory bread
pudding with baby artichokes; in meat
pâtés, mayonnaise, and vichyssoise; and
in a green aioli sauce. Sorrel's best-
known use is in a rich French soup.

# SWEET WOODRUFF
## *Galium odoratum*

THIS FRAGRANT PLANT IS KNOWN especially for its traditional use in May wine.

**How to grow:** Sweet woodruff's dark green foliage and tiny white flowers make an attractive ground cover in shade. The plant seldom grows higher than a foot and is hardy to USDA Zone 3. As its seeds are slow to germinate, it is usually propagated by division or transplants. Sweet woodruff prefers partial to full shade and rich, well-drained soil.

The German name for woodruff is *Waldmeister*, which literally means

Mexican tarragon

Sweet woodruff

"Master of the forest." There it grows wild in the deep shade of pine forests. Traditionally the fragrant herb is collected just before it blooms, usually in the month of May, to make May wine. You may want to restrain it, as it is self-sowing and can become a weed. Mowing will help control sweet woodruff but will not harm it.

**How to prepare:** Sweet woodruff has a faint vanilla fragrance that is stronger when the plant is wilted or dried. Pick the stems and dry them upside down in bunches. Sweet woodruff freezes well. The flowers can be used in salads. Fresh or dry leaves are used in tea or in May wine. In Germany one also finds this herb used as a flavoring for a gelatin dessert and a lovely syrup that is used to create the famous wheat beer, Berliner Weisse.

# TARRAGON
## *Artemisia dracunculus*

TARRAGON, SOMETIMES CALLED FRENCH tarragon, is a rich but delicately flavored herb with an anisey flavor. *Tagetes lucida*, variously called Mexican tarragon, Mexican mint marigold, and sweet marigold is a more assertive herb, but it has a similar flavor.

**How to grow:** French tarragon is a perennial hardy to USDA Zone 4 that grows to about two feet. The plant is started from divisions, never from seeds, and in the extremes of the coldest and hottest humid climates it must be started anew every spring. Happily, gardeners in the South can grow Mexican tarragon instead. This tender perennial is hardy only to USDA Zone

8, grows to about three feet, and has yellow flowers in late fall. It is semi-evergreen in the mildest winters but dies back to the ground if it freezes. Grow both tarragons in full sun (though they can tolerate some afternoon shade) and in rich, very well drained soil. Water the plants moderately throughout the growing season. When ordering plants, do not confuse French with Russian tarragon, which is much inferior in flavor and is sometimes sold as seeds. Both French and Mexican tarragons need to be divided every few years to keep them growing vigorously. They have few pests, but French tarragon has occasional problems with root rot and mildew.

**How to prepare:** Harvest leaves of both French and Mexican tarragons and use fresh anytime during the growing season. The French tarragon flavor does not preserve well, but if you want to try, put the leaves in vinegar or freeze them. The Mexican tarragon dries fairly well. French tarragon adds richness and a slight anise flavor to sauces, particularly béarnaise sauce, and salad dressings; and the French have used it in omelets and on poultry, fish, and veal for centuries. Mexican tarragon has an affinity for corn, squash, tomatoes, and turkey. Use both tarragons sparingly, as the flavor can overpower a dish.

French tarragon

French tarragon

'Lime,' 'French,' and 'Wooly' thyme

# THYME

## *Thymus* spp.

THYME IS VERSATILE in the garden and the kitchen and is used in cuisines throughout the world.

**How to grow:** These spreading perennials vary from four to twelve inches in height and have either gray-green, dark green, golden, or silver foliage, depending on the variety. Some are more useful in the landscape, while others are more useful in the kitchen. French thyme, *T. vulgaris,* is the most commonly used culinary thyme. Other choice varieties are lemon thyme, *T. x citriodorus*, which has a rich lemon taste and pink flowers; caraway thyme, *T. herba-barona,* with a caraway taste, dark green leaves, and pink flowers; and 'Orange Balsam,' which has an orange flavor and is a favorite of West

bination with most herbs for a more complex flavor. In fact, except for lemon thyme, I seldom use thyme alone. Small amounts of thyme complement many vegetables and most meat and fish dishes, soups, stews, salad dressing, and marinades. Thyme is one ingredient of the traditional French *bouquet garni* and also of *herbes de Provence.* Try slipping a little lemon thyme under the skin of poultry before roasting or add it to mint tea. Thyme leaves can be dried as is or preserved in vinegar or oil.

Indians. All the thymes need full sun and fast-draining soil. Most thymes are hardy to USDA Zone 5, but in cold-winter areas they need protective mulches. In spring cut back the foliage by about one-third so the plant will stay lush. In mild climates many light prunings are needed during the growing season. Most gardeners start plants with transplants or by cuttings, though occasionally from seeds. Thymes are quite pest- and disease-resistant.

**How to prepare:** Thyme can be harvested anytime throughout the growing season. It is wonderful fresh, though stripping the leaves off the stems can be tedious. Simplify the process by drying the stems until just brittle and then gently rubbing them between your palms to remove the leaves. Like parsley, thyme is a complementary herb and can be used in com-

French thyme

# favorite herb recipes

I have an amber jar of magic in my refrigerator. It's a marinade of olive oil crammed full of garlic and fresh basil leaves. When I add a spoonful of this oil to an omelet or a soup, I feel like Tinker Bell spreading magic dust. Presto! The dish explodes with flavor. Everyday foods become instant decadence. I spread this flavored oil on toast or in the pan before I cook potatoes. I use it in a salad or on green beans and zucchini. Sometimes I make herb butters, other times herb vinegar instead. And I use other herbs—maybe 'Cinnamon' basil, tarragon, or lemon thyme. To quote my grandmother, at any one time I have an elegant sufficiency of herbs.

Growing fresh herbs gives you the luxury of doing a little "show-off cooking." Sprigs of red basil, curly and flat-leaf parsley, sage, flowers of wild marjoram and chives, and the edible flowers of runner beans and violas are arranged to create showy canapés.

Like most Americans, I grew up with few herbs in my food, and the ones I did know were dried. According to the late French chef Tom McCombie, "We Americans are so used to seeing our herbs labeled 'Schilling' or 'McCormick' that we expect them to be grown in the cans we buy them in. Most of us have no idea that basil and tarragon in their fresh form bear no resemblance to the dried products. In fact, many of our cookbooks call for 'tarragon' or 'parsley' and 'chervil' or 'parsley.' Well, they're all green, but

that's really where the resemblance ends. In France, I worked in some of the greatest restaurants and I never once saw a can of herbs. I feel that's one of the main reasons French food is so good." Today, with a garden full of herbs, I know now that I grew up not color-blind but "herb-blind."

## "Painting" with Garden Herbs

If you are new to herb gardening, a good way to begin learning about herbs is to think of a garden containing a dozen varieties of fresh herbs as a kind of palette of paints to work with in the kitchen. As with colors, the possibilities are endless. You can choose your medium and then the herb, or just the reverse. It's really hard to go wrong. Here are some ways to get started. But remember that in

Assertive herbs such as fennel, sage, rosemary, and oregano stand up well to the bold flavors of garlic and chile peppers.

favorite in southern parts of Europe, is often flavored with basil, thyme, oregano, fennel, or parsley. The famous peas of the English are served with mint, and in other parts of the world cooks use thyme, chervil, and basil with their peas.

The sweetness of peppers combines naturally with the strong tastes of basil, oregano, or thyme; spinach is complemented by dill or basil in an omelet. Also try a dill-and-feta-cheese filling for filo-dough pastries or in crêpes. Certain vegetables seem to have been created as vehicles for herb flavors— namely, potatoes, tomatoes, and summer squash. Try potatoes mashed or baked and sprinkled with parsley, tarragon, dill, chervil, or thyme; or roast them with rosemary or sage. And have tomatoes or summer squash with basil, oregano, parsley, thyme, fennel, anise seeds, mint, bay, cilantro, borage, rosemary, tarragon, or cumin.

Of course, other foodstuffs are also good vehicles for herbs. Take breads, for instance. I've already described my method of spreading olive oil seasoned with basil and garlic on toast. Also try adding fresh dill to your white bread

most cases fresh herbs are preferred over dried.

Let's begin with the medium of vegetables. For asparagus, try adding some chopped fresh dill leaves or tarragon to the mayonnaise you serve it with. When you cook snap beans, add a little fresh chopped savory, basil, dill, or tarragon to the pan. If you are cooking dry beans in a recipe, add some thyme, oregano, basil, or savory, and for Mexican-style black beans, epazote.

A brief overview of the world's cuisines turns up a wealth of simple, time-tested ideas. In Germany, for instance, beets are sometimes served with caraway or dill, particularly if they are pickled. You might also want to try adding lemon balm. For eons people have enjoyed cabbage cooked with caraway, dill, mint, or sage. The neutral flavors of the cabbage seem to soak up herb flavors readily. In France sweet, young carrots are often seasoned with dill, mint, chervil, thyme, or tarragon; and all over Europe cucumbers are flavored with dill, chervil, tarragon, or basil. In the Middle East cucumbers are combined with mint, and in India with cilantro. Eggplant, a

TIP:

Most of us are trying to cut down on salt in our diet and fresh herbs provide a flavorful alternative. Instead of adding salt to, say, a vegetable soup or steamed beans, try a last-minute sprinkle of chopped fresh basil, dill, or tarragon.

or potato bread dough before baking. Or add sage to your biscuit dough when you make dumplings, rosemary on top of focaccia, and use basil in your cornbread.

Herbs have many uses, of course, with meats and fish of all types. Herbs add a new dimension to marinades—try one made of Italian seasonings on a London broil or hamburgers. Marinate pork in a sauce with sage, or chicken in a sauce with fennel. And sprinkle rosemary on lamb chops before putting them on the barbecue. A light sauce for fish is exquisite with just a hint of dill or chervil. A lamb stew is much more interesting when a handful of fresh chopped mint is added. Add chopped herbs of all types to hamburg-

ers before cooking, or sprinkle them over a chicken before baking it. Also glazes made with herbs and jelly or mustard will spice up the blandest meat dishes.

Cheeses and egg dishes respond gloriously to fresh herbs. Layering soft cheese with chopped herbs makes a fancy but easy hors d'oeuvre. Fill omelets and soufflés with fresh herbs and build a special brunch around baked eggs served with a sauce containing chopped dill or tarragon. Or try eggs Benedict with an herbed hollandaise.

Garnishes make up another medium. Use sprigs of fresh dill or fennel with fish, and place the beautiful leaves of golden sage around a tea sandwich

tray. Sprigs of mint are nice in cold drinks and fruit salads. Teas too constitute a medium for fresh herbs. In particular, try the mints and the lemon- and anise-flavored herbs.

In the following section I've assembled many ways to feature the flavors of all types of herbs in combination, both fresh and dried, and in infusions of all types, and I have included many ways to preserve the essence of an herb for the winter.

Lavender sprigs give honey a subtle but rich flavor. Steep the sprigs in the honey then strain it. The fragrant honey can be drizzled over garden raspberries served with crème fraîche.

# featuring herbal flavors

# Fresh Herb Blends

The French are fond of herbs, and starting with a few French classics is a lovely way to begin. *Bouquet garni* and *fines herbes* are such versatile herb mixes, we've all probably used variations without calling them by their official titles. Bouquet garni is used to infuse a soup, stock, or sauce with complex flavors. Herbs are tied together with aromatic vegetables, added at the beginning of cooking, and removed at the end.

## Bouquet Garni

1 small leek, or large leek sliced
    lengthwise, white part only
1 carrot
2 celery ribs, with greens
1 sprig fresh lovage
3 sprigs fresh parsley
3 sprigs fresh thyme
1 bay leaf

Tie all the ingredients together with clean white string. Leave a tail on the string so you can secure it to the pot and remove it easily.

## Fines Herbes

*Fines herbes* is a mixture of chopped herbs. You will see dried mixes labeled "fines herbes," but the elusive flavors of the primary herbs—tarragon, parsley, and chervil—fade when dried. The traditional mixture calls for equal amounts of minced fresh parsley, tarragon, chervil, and chives or thyme. This mix is added at the last minute to soups, sauces, vinaigrettes, and savory egg dishes.

## Gremolata

Here's another traditional herb blend—this one from Italy. It adds a "wallop" of flavor when sprinkled over osso buco, roast lamb, baked chicken, and fish; when added to soups before serving; or when stirred into marinades and sauces.

1 large lemon
½ cup chopped fresh Italian
    parsley
1 small garlic clove, minced
⅛ teaspoon salt
Dash of freshly ground black
    pepper

Grate the lemon peel. Place it in a small bowl, and mix in the parsley, garlic, salt, and pepper. It will keep for three days in the refrigerator.
Makes ⅔ cup.

A basic green salad can be given many faces by changing the selection of fresh herbs. Here are a number of fresh herb salad blends.

## Tangy Herb Blend

This blend is wonderful over a salad of mixed lettuces and tomatoes with a basic vinaigrette.

12 to 16 fresh sorrel leaves,
    chopped
2 tablespoons chopped fresh
    parsley
3 tablespoons fresh burnet leaves

## Asian Herb Blend

This herb mix can be used in a salad—try making the vinaigrette with rice wine vinegar and a little soy sauce, and add grilled scallops to the salad. This blend can also be added to a stir-fry at the end of cooking.

- 2 tablespoons chopped fresh cilantro
- 2 teaspoons minced fresh lemongrass
- 1 tablespoon finely snipped fresh Oriental chives

## Classic Mesclun Herb Blend

Mesclun salad mixes are great from the garden and are now available in many markets. Traditionally, fresh herbs are included in the salad. Add the following herb blend to your mesclun next time and see what you think.

- 2 tablespoons chopped fresh chervil
- 1 tablespoon chopped fresh thyme
- 1 tablespoon chopped fresh tarragon

## Fresh Flavor Herb Blend

Another herb variation adds dimension to vegetable salads. Try it on tomatoes and cucumbers, with avocados and root vegetables, or added to risotto.

- 1 tablespoon snipped fresh dill
- 2 teaspoons chopped fresh borage
- 1 tablespoon snipped fresh chives

## Summer Essence Herb Blend

Use the following blend in tomato soup, on pizza, in a green or bean salad, or in just about any dish with lots of tomatoes.

- 2 tablespoons chopped fresh basil
- 2 teaspoons chopped fresh tarragon
- 1 tablespoon chopped fresh parsley

Featured here (*below*) are the work horses of the herb garden: flat-leaf and curly parsley, sage, rosemary, and French and lemon thyme. Use them in butters, pasta sauces, salad dressings, vegetable soups, poultry stuffings, meat stews, and in a marinade for roast meats.

Even a garden with only a half dozen herb plants produces enough to share. Before a party, gather up little bouquets of fresh herbs, tie them with raffia, and take them to your host and hostess. Or dry the herbs in small quantities and give them as a bridal shower gift. For a festive presentation, put the dry herbs in a basket and add a great bottle of olive oil, a fancy vinegar, and your favorite salad dressing recipe.

# Dry Herb Blends

Drying herbs not only preserves the flavor for the off-season but sometimes can enhance the flavor as well. Many of the following blends have many variations under the same name, such as the classic *herbes de Provence*.

## Herbes de Provence

In looking through French reference books, I found many different blends, all called *herbes de Provence*. The ones I gravitate toward are from Jacques Pépin and Antoine Bouterin. Other chefs add savory or sweet marjoram to the blend. According to Pépin, his blend is equal parts dried thyme, sage, rosemary, lavender, and fennel seeds. Use the blend with red meats and vegetables.

### Herbes de Provence à la Bouterin

4 tablespoons dried thyme
2 tablespoons dried rosemary
1 tablespoon dried lavender
1 tablespoon fennel seeds
3 bay leaves, crushed

## Tex-Mex Hot Barbecue Blend

A blend from a spicy part of the world, this mixture is great rubbed on beef, chicken, and pork before barbecuing. This recipe is for the "hot-heads"; if you don't like your food blazing, omit the chile Piquín.

2 tablespoons crumbled, dried Mexican oregano
1 tablespoon cumin seeds, toasted and ground
1 teaspoon chile Piquín flakes
1 teaspoon chili powder

## Fresh Light Blend

Use this blend for poultry stuffing, in a lemon butter over fish, and added to soups.

2 tablespoons dried lemon thyme
1 tablespoon dried rosemary
1 tablespoon dried Greek oregano

## Roast Potato Blend

2 tablespoons dried sweet marjoram
2 tablespoons dried thyme

For a delicious potato dish, parboil approximately 24 small potatoes (or 1½ pounds) until they're almost tender. Put them in a shallow baking pan to which 3 tablespoons of olive oil has been added, and stir to coat them. Sprinkle salt and pepper and the herb blend over them and stir again. Bake at 400° F, stirring occasionally until golden brown. (Bake about 20 to 30 minutes.)

## Roasted Root Vegetable Blend

Here's another roasting mix; you can use it interchangeably with the Roast Potato Blend.

1 tablespoon dried rosemary
½ tablespoon dried savory
½ tablespoon dried thyme

## Roasted Root Vegetables with Herbs

Serve these vegetables warm to accompany an omelet, meats, and fish or serve them at room temperature over a green salad or as a stand-alone buffet dish.

2 pounds mixed root vegetables such as carrots, golden beets, parsnips, and turnips cut into 1-inch-diameter pieces
2 pounds new potatoes, about 1 inch wide, or larger ones cut into 1-inch pieces
3 tablespoons extra-virgin olive oil
Dash of salt
¼ teaspoon freshly ground black pepper
1 recipe Roasted Root Vegetable Blend
6 garlic cloves, chopped
3 tablespoons balsamic vinegar

Preheat oven to 350° F. It's important that the vegetables be the same size, so they'll cook at the same rate. Place them in a roasting pan approximately 10 inches by 13 inches and drizzle on the olive oil, season with salt and pepper, and stir to distribute the oil. Smooth out the vegetables into an even layer. Bake for 1 hour, stirring occasionally so they cook evenly. Remove the pan from the oven and sprinkle the herb blend and garlic over the vegetables and stir. Return the pan to the oven and bake for another 45 minutes or so, or until tender. Remove from the oven, sprinkle on the balsamic vinegar, and stir.

Serves 4.

# Pestos

Pesto is generally defined as a paste of olive oil, garlic, nuts, Parmesan cheese, and fresh basil and is a specialty of the area around Genoa, Italy. It is served as a sauce for pasta or is used as a flavoring for soup. But many modern chefs adhere to a more general definition, making a pesto with cilantro, peanuts, and peanut oil; mint with corn oil and walnuts; or even dry, without oil. The dry pesto has fewer applications, but again, it is a way to preserve that fresh flavor. Pestos are versatile as toppings for pizza, pastas, stews, and soups. Most can be incorporated into sauces for meats and mixed with yogurt, mayonnaise, or sour cream into dressings for salads. Finally, pesto freezes well and is a way to preserve the herb's flavor after the season is past. The following recipes are for a classic basil pesto and a dry rosemary pesto. They may be frozen in small canning jars and kept for four to six months. When freezing, leave out the cheese and add it just before serving. To prevent discoloration, place plastic wrap directly on the surface of the pesto before you freeze it.

All sorts of herbs can be used to make pesto. Rosemary is ideal for making a dry pesto to serve on minestrone soup or over a rich lamb stew.

### Classic Pesto

Serve this pesto over fettuccine, or other pasta, either dry or fresh. Try combining cooked green snap beans with the noodles for a lovely variation.

- 3 garlic cloves
- 2 cups fresh basil leaves
- ¼ cup pine nuts or walnuts
- ½ teaspoon salt
- ¼ teaspoon freshly ground black pepper
- ¾ cup extra-virgin olive oil
- ½ cup freshly grated Parmesan cheese

In a blender or food processor, combine the garlic, basil leaves, nuts, salt, pepper, and half the oil. Puree, slowly adding the remaining oil. Transfer the mixture to a bowl and add the grated cheese, mixing thoroughly. Use immediately or cover with plastic wrap, since basil pesto turns brown if exposed to air. If you are going to serve this pesto over pasta, you may need to add a few tablespoons of cooking water to the pesto to make it the right consistency for the pasta.

Makes approximately 1¼ cups.

### Rosemary Pesto

Sometimes I make this pesto in a blender, but I find I must mince the garlic and finely chop the rosemary, or they don't blend properly. This pesto is added to a minestrone or tomato soup or sprinkled over a pizza before baking.

- 3 large garlic cloves, minced
- Handful of fresh Italian parsley leaves
- Leaves from 2 (3-inch) sprigs of fresh rosemary
- 6 tablespoons freshly grated Parmesan cheese
- ½ dried hot pepper

In a mortar, put the garlic, parsley, rosemary, Parmesan cheese, and hot pepper. Pound the ingredients with the pestle to a crumbly paste and serve.

Makes about ½ cup.

## Herb Vinegars

The flavors of many herbs are lost when the herbs are dried, but they can be preserved effectively in another form. Use white wine or rice wine vinegar for the milder herbs, and red wine vinegar for assertive herbs like oregano and rosemary. This method works well for dill, tarragon, thyme, lemon thyme, the basils ('Red Rubin' basil gives a beautiful magenta hue to vinegar, and 'Cinnamon' and 'Anise' basils impart pinkish tones), mint, or your favorite combinations. You may add other flavorings, such as garlic, onion, chives, hot peppers, or spices. If you want to make the vinegar in quantities for giving as gifts, you can buy vinegar at institutional supply houses in gallon jugs.

Use these herb-flavored vinegars in salad dressings, for marinades, in soups, or in just about any dish in which you would use unflavored vinegar. Try a mint vinegar in fruit salad or a tarragon vinegar in potato salad. Herb vinegars will store for up to a year.

### Red Rubin Basil Vinegar

2 handfuls of roughly chopped
  fresh Red Rubin basil
4 garlic cloves, roughly chopped
1 pint white wine vinegar

Pack the basil loosely in a large, wide-mouthed pint jar (the stems and flowers can go in along with the leaves) and add the garlic. Fill the jar with vinegar. Cover and leave the jar in a dark place for one to two months. Strain the infusion through cheesecloth or a fine sieve, and then pour it through a funnel into bottles (clear glass shows off the colors best; use pretty bottles for holiday gifts), leaving any sediment at the bottom of the jar. Decorate the bottles with a sprig of the herb you used for flavoring, and then seal the tops.

Makes 1 pint.

## Herb Oils

Oils are wonderful vehicles for herb flavors, and just about any oil will suffice. The best herbs for using in oils are sweet basil, lemon basil, dill, rosemary, tarragon, thyme, and lemon thyme. Use herb oils in salad dressings or as a substitute for butter on steamed vegetables such as carrots, zucchini,

Preserving in vinegar is one of the best ways to keep the flavor of basil over the winter. Use a wide-mouth jar to make it easy to add the herbs and garlic.

beans, broccoli, and cauliflower. Herb oil is also wonderful on toasted bread or as a chief ingredient in potato salad. Try dill oil drizzled over carrots or cucumbers, and basil or tarragon oil on tomatoes, zucchini, peppers, and potatoes. Lemon thyme oil is great over broccoli, carrots, cauliflower, and fish or chicken.

*Caution:* Storing at room temperature any oil with herbs or other foodstuffs in them can cause botulism. It is critical that herb oils be stored in the refrigerator.

### Tarragon Oil

Two large handfuls (approximately 2 cups) roughly chopped fresh tarragon
1 dry hot pepper (optional)
1 pint pure virgin olive oil

In a sterile pint jar, place the tarragon and hot pepper (if desired). Cover it with olive oil, making sure that you have at least 1 inch of oil on top of the herbs. Refrigerate for 10 days. (The olive oil will solidify, but it reliquifies after a few minutes at room temperature.) After 10 days bring the oil to room temperature and strain. Discard the tarragon and hot pepper. Store the now completed oil in the refrigerator; it will keep for up to two weeks.

**Note:** For safety reasons always remember to refrigerate your herb oils. In the refrigerator olive oil solidifies but soon becomes liquid again at room temperature.

Many types of herb oils can be used to dress a salad.

# Herb Teas

Chamomile, spearmint, and peppermint are all familiar herbs for tea, but pineapple sage, ginger mint, lemon-verbena, rosemary, fennel, and lemongrass make wonderful teas as well. Herb teas can be combined with white grape and apple juice and may be steeped with dried lemon or orange peel, ginger, anise seeds, and cloves to make more complex teas. Of course, individual herbs can be used, or you can combine herbs.

Herb teas can be made with either fresh or dried herbs and can be served either hot or cold. The general proportions are 1 teaspoon dried herbs to 1 cup water versus 1 tablespoon fresh herbs to 1 cup water. When making iced teas, double the amount of herbs, as the tea will be diluted with the melting ice.

To make a perfect cup of hot herb tea, first rinse the teapot with boiling water. Add the herbs, adding an extra teaspoonful for the pot, and pour in boiling water. Cover the pot and let it sit for 3 to 5 minutes. If it steeps too long, the tea gets bitter. Pour the hot tea out through a strainer into cups. Serve with sugar or honey and lemon.

### Chamomile Cooler

Chamomile is most beloved as a soothing herb tea. The following is Wendy Krupnick's iced variation that helps cool a hot day.

- 1 heaping tablespoon dried German chamomile
- 1 heaping tablespoon crushed, dried spearmint or peppermint leaves
- 1 quart apple juice
- 1 tablespoon lemon or lime juice (optional)
- Garnish: lemon slices and fresh mint leaves

Place the herbs in an ovenproof jar or pot. Pour 3 cups of boiling water over the herbs, cover the pot, and let it steep for 15 to 20 minutes. Strain the tea into a large pitcher. Add the apple juice and lemon or lime juice (if desired) and chill. Serve over ice and garnish.

Serves 6.

### May Wine Bowl

This recipe is from Rose Marie Nichols McGee of Nichols Garden Nursery in Albany, Oregon, and it is a variation on the traditional libation from Germany. Germans use this traditional punch to celebrate May Day. In Germany sweet woodruff grows wild in the woods and is collected before it flowers, to capture the best taste. Germans use only wilted or dry sweet woodruff and add champagne or sparkling water.

- 5 bottles Moselle or Riesling wine
- 2 large handfuls sweet woodruff, cleaned
- 1 cup brandy
- 1 cup sugar
- A large ring mold of ice
- 1 cup strawberries, Alpine or wild, if available

Pour 2 bottles of the wine into a large jar or crock, add 2 large handfuls of dry or wilted sweet woodruff, cover and refrigerate, and let stand for 3 days. Strain the infused wine into a large punch bowl and add the remaining 3 bottles of wine and the brandy, sugar, and ice. Add the strawberries to the bowl and decorate around the base of the bowl with sweet woodruff.

Serves about 20.

# Herb Butter

Serve this savory butter with a crisp French bread or melted over vegetables, fish, poultry, or a classic filet mignon. The butter can be rolled out between sheets of waxed paper and then cut into shapes with a very small cookie cutter. Here I have used tarragon, but chives, lemon thyme, rosemary, basil, or a combination of herbs can be used.

# Herb Cream

**N**obody can boast of the health aspects of cream, but it sure does taste good. Add mint to the cream, whip it to serve with chocolate cake, steep it with savory for a sauce for potatoes and leeks, or steep it with basil and add it to custard. Flavored creams are the greatest.

### Mint Whipped Cream

¼ cup chopped fresh spearmint
    or peppermint
1½ cups whipping cream
1½ tablespoons granulated sugar
¼ teaspoon vanilla extract

Place the mint and cream in a small saucepan over a low heat until small bubbles just begin to form around the sides of the pan. Do not let the cream boil. Cool. Pour the cream through a mesh strainer and discard the mint. Chill.

Just before serving, place the cream in a mixing bowl and whip it until the cream just starts to hold its shape. Add the sugar slowly as you mix. Add the vanilla and continue to whip until soft peaks form.

Makes 1½ cups.

### Tarragon Butter

4 ounces (1 stick) unsalted butter
    at room temperature
2 tablespoons minced fresh
    tarragon
½ teaspoon lemon zest
1 tablespoon lemon juice

Cut the stick of butter in 6 or 8 pieces and then mash the butter with a fork to soften it. When it's fairly soft, slowly incorporate the tarragon, lemon zest, and lemon juice. Use a rubber spatula to transfer the mixture to a small bowl. Refrigerate until serving time.

Makes ½ cup.

# the Saville herb garden

The first time I visited San Francisco Bay Area resident Carole Saville, she lived in Los Angeles, and I went to see her herb garden. As we chatted, she offered me some herb tea. I expected her to get out a jar of dried herbs, but instead she stepped out of her kitchen door and gathered some fresh leaves of lemongrass and peppermint. Her teapot was glass, and when she put the leaves in it and poured boiling water over them, I could see the water turn bright green. That cup of tea I drank with honey was the best I had ever tasted.

When the time came to prepare dinner, out Carole went to her herb garden again, this time to gather snippets of tarragon and winter savory. She proceeded to slip the tarragon under the skins of Cornish game hens and chop the winter savory and put it in with the snap beans. When dinner was about ready, she went out once more to gather some crisp, fresh herbs and a few edible flowers for the salad. The meal had such richness and there were so many flavors woven through it from course to course that I realized, not for the first or last time, that I had a great deal to learn about herbs.

Since that day fifteen years ago, Carole has become even more involved with herbs. When I first met her, she was writing about cuisine, styling food for photographs, and giving seminars on herbs. Carole continues to devote herself full-time to the exploration of herbs, writing about them for magazines and books, including her latest books, *Exotic Herbs* and *Herbs*.

When Carole and I agreed that I would use her garden in my book, I asked her for some background, starting with how she had become interested in herbs. She told me that when she moved from New York City to a wonderful old house in New Jersey, she and her

Carole Saville gathers herbs in her Los Angeles herb garden.

husband, Brent, decided to put in an herb garden because of her interest in cooking. After a few years she actually ended up with three herb gardens. The first was an informal one filled with culinary herbs, the next was an ornamental herb garden containing primarily plants with blue flowers, and the third was a traditional English knot garden.

Eventually, Carole and Brent moved to Los Angeles. On their cross-country flight they brought cuttings of some of Carole's favorite herbs, and they quickly installed them in a new herb garden. It was designed in a classic geometric pattern with a raised brick planter in the middle. And, of course, it was right off the kitchen. Today, because Carole is so busy writing, she has limited herself to one herb garden. It contains all the culinary herbs she finds indispensable, including all the popular ones, such as thyme, basil, and sage, and less common ones like sweet cicely, salad burnet, and nepitella. Recently her interest has turned to the many cultivars of traditional herbs, such as 'Golden Rain' rosemary,

'African Blue' basil, and 'Bronze' perilla, and many new herbs introduced by Southeast Asians. For instance, she likes to combine lemongrass and Vietnamese balm in a subtle, fragrant lemonade, and cilantro and Thai basil in chicken salad.

I asked Carole to describe a few of her favorite ways of cooking with herbs. "I like to use generous amounts of chopped fresh thyme, marjoram, parsley, and dill in rice for herbed rice," she began. "And I enjoy serving herb butters made with parsley and capers, or *fines herbes* with crusty breads. I slip leaves of basil, tarragon, or oregano under the skin of chicken before I bake it. I substitute cilantro for basil in pesto and chop rosemary or sage up fine and add it to my cornbread batter before baking it. Lemongrass, roselle (*Hibiscus sabdariffa*), and spearmint I use in teas; and I make a 'Meyer' lemon confiture [jelly] flavored with English lavender or lemon verbena. Sometimes I rub the salad bowl with lovage before I add the greens, to give the salad a celery taste, and I often add basil or chervil

to mayonnaise or add chopped herbs to the dressing. I could go on and on. I just can't imagine cooking without my herb garden."

## Herbed Vodka

I was surprised to learn that Carole also uses herbs in more unique ways: to flavor vodkas, for example. I had never heard of flavored vodkas before, but Carole quickly brought me up to date on them.

"Flavored vodkas are ones that have either herbs, spices, or fruits added to them," she explained. "They first became popular in old Russia, where distillation and filtering methods were crude and something was needed to mask the tastes. The solution? Flavoring the liquor with fruits, berries, or herbs. In fact, Peter the Great habitually peppered his vodka, a practice thought to draw impurities to the bottom of the glass.

"Flavored vodkas are very popular in Eastern Europe today," Carole said. Old World favorites include *pertsovka*, reputedly Stalin's favorite, which has the spicy taste of hot peppers; *okhotnichya*, or hunter's vodka, flavored with herbs and berries; and *chesnochnaya*, vodka infused with garlic, dill, and peppercorns.

While Russians drink flavored vodka throughout a meal, commonly referring to it as "the little ray of sunshine in the stomach," Carole likes to serve it with the first course—a nice way to begin a meal, she says. And while imported flavored vodkas are available in the United States from ethnic markets catering to Eastern Europeans, Carole recommends making your own. Commercial vodkas taste much stronger and certainly are not as fresh as homemade, and you can create your own combinations when you make them yourself.

When I asked Carole which flavors she likes best, she said, "I personally like to flavor vodka with mint, rosemary, or sweet woodruff, or with edible flowers such as roses, lavender, or dianthus—alone or in combinations. But I think everyone should be an alchemist and experiment in the kitchen!

"I use only good-quality Polish, Russian, or Swedish vodka," Carole emphasized, "because the primary flavor is still vodka. I put herbs in the vodka and keep it at room temperature for a day or two.

"Chefs and vodka aficionados have different opinions as to how long to infuse the herbs to achieve the best fragrance; the vodka will take on the flavor in just one day, but I like to leave it a little longer. Whatever your taste, the vodka is best if stored in a freezer because the liquid thickens slightly and the flavors become more pronounced.

"I save pretty bottles, about sixteen-ounce capacity, to transfer the vodka into when it's ready. I serve the vodka ice cold in ice-cold glasses with smoked salmon or other smoked fish or—if the pocketbook allows—caviar."

Carole likes to serve vodka in small, pretty glasses that she buys in antique shops. If the glasses are mismatched, she says, all the better. She prefers small glasses because they hold only small amounts; she thinks vodka should be sipped, and the smaller amount prevents people from getting drunk. As Carole said, "Drinking flavored vodkas, like using flavored vinegars and oils, is a way to enjoy the fresh taste of some of humanity's favorite herb flavors."

Herb and flower vodkas (*left*) made with roses, lemongrass, dianthus, English lavender, kumquats, sweet woodruff, and costmary. Serve them ice cold. Here's Carole's recipe for

### Flavored Vodkas

2 cups good-quality vodka

1 tablespoon sweet woodruff leaves, *or*
    2 tablespoons fresh lemongrass stalks cut diagonally from the white portion of the base into ¼-inch slices, *or* 1 teaspoon coarsely chopped, fresh, English lavender

Combine the herbs and vodka in a very clean wide-mouth pint jar. Seal the jar and allow the mixture to steep for 24 hours at room temperature. Taste for flavoring. If a stronger flavor is desired, infuse the herbs for another 24 hours, or until the flavor suits you. Strain the mixture through a cheesecloth-lined funnel, and pour it into a very clean, decorative pint bottle. Seal tightly with a cork or cap. Store the flavored vodka in the freezer.

    Makes 2 cups.

# Gudi's Potato Pancakes with Chives

In some parts of Germany these pancakes are made with grated onions. Here Gudi Riter, my kitchen assistant, used chives for a milder flavor and for their lovely green snippets of color. In Germany these pancakes are traditionally served with applesauce for a brunch or lunch. They are best eaten immediately out of the pan, when they are still hot and crisp.

2 pounds Yukon Gold or Yellow
    Fins potatoes, peeled
1 medium-size onion, peeled
½ cup snipped fresh chives
2 eggs
3 tablespoons all-purpose flour

1 teaspoon salt
Freshly ground pepper and
    nutmeg
Vegetable oil
Garnish: chive blossoms

Finely grate the potatoes. (The best texture is achieved by using the second-smallest grater on a four-sided hand grater. The opening is less than ⅛ inch.) When grated, the potatoes will almost have the consistency of paste. Place the grated potatoes in a fine sieve or cheesecloth for about 15 minutes, to allow as much liquid as possible to drain. Squeeze the potatoes with your hands to extract more moisture if the mixture is still runny. (Some potatoes have more liquid than others.) When dry enough, the potato paste will more or less form a loose ball. Grate the onion using the same grater size.

In a mixing bowl, mix well the potato paste, grated onion, chives, and eggs. Add the flour, salt, pepper, and nutmeg to taste, and mix again.

In a large frying pan, add enough oil to cover the bottom of the pan to a depth of about ⅛ inch. Heat the oil over medium heat. With a tablespoon, put a generous dollop of batter into the pan and flatten it with the back of the spoon to about the size of the palm of your hand. Fry the pancakes, three or four at a time until golden brown on both sides (approximately 3 minutes per side). Remove the potato pancakes from the pan and drain them on paper towels. Serve immediately with a garnish of chive blossoms. Makes 12 to 14 small pancakes.

Serves 2 or 3 as a side dish, more as an appetizer.

# Salmon, Cream Cheese, and Chive Torta

This stylish dish is great for a Sunday brunch served with bagels or as part of a buffet accompanied by crusty bread. The final flavor and texture of the dish depend on using good natural cream cheese, with no added gums, and choosing flavorful smoked salmon.

1 pound natural cream cheese

½ cup plus 2 tablespoons snipped fresh chives

½ cup finely chopped smoked salmon

In a small bowl, crumble half of the cream cheese, add ½ cup of the chives, and mix together with a fork. If necessary, add a few teaspoons of water to hold the mixture together and make it spreadable. Do not make it too soft, or the torta will not hold its shape.

To shape the torta, drape a small piece of cheesecloth to line a 2½- to 3-cup mold or straight-sided bowl. With a rubber spatula, form the bottom layer by spreading the chive and cream cheese mixture in the bottom of the mold, smoothing it out and filling any air holes.

In another bowl, crumble the remaining cream cheese and work in the salmon by repeating the procedure just outlined. Spread the salmon mixture on top of the chive mixture.

To unmold the torta, place a small serving plate facedown on top of the mold, making sure the cheesecloth is free of the plate and that the mold is centered on the plate. Hold the plate tightly against the top of the torta and turn the mold over. Lift off the mold and gently peel off the cheesecloth. To garnish, sprinkle the remaining 2 tablespoons of chives over the top.

Serves 6 to 8.

TIP:

The best way to cut chives is to snip them with scissors. If you have extra chopped chives put them in a small self-sealing freezer bag and freeze them. They can be added directly to marinades and cooked dishes in the winter and won't need defrosting.

# Fancy Carrot and Onion Soup

This is a world-class soup! The sweet, bright flavors of carrots contrast beautifully with the dusky flavors of the lovage, coriander, and parsley in the onion soup garnish. The presentation is most dramatic if you serve the soup in individual shallow bowls.

4 cups sliced carrots

2 tablespoons vegetable oil

2 cups chopped onion

1 garlic clove, finely chopped

1½ cups chicken broth

⅔ cup half-and-half, divided

1 tablespoon coriander or cumin seeds

2 stalks fresh lovage or fresh Italian parsley

Garnish: small sprigs of dill or lovage, or carrot leaves

**To make the carrot soup:**

Steam the carrots until tender. In a large pan, heat the oil and sauté the onions until translucent, add the garlic, and sauté 1 more minute. In a food processor or blender, puree the onion mixture. Transfer ½ cup of the onion puree to a small saucepan and set it aside. Leave the remaining onion mixture in the food processor.

Add the steamed carrots to the food processor and blend until smooth. Transfer the mixture to a saucepan, add the chicken broth, stir, and simmer 1 minute. Remove the carrot soup from the heat and set it aside.

**To make the onion soup:**

In a dry, heavy frying pan, lightly toast the coriander or cumin seeds—keep stirring to prevent them from burning. In a saucepan, heat ⅓ cup of the half-and-half, add the toasted coriander or cumin seeds and the lovage or Italian parsley. Remove from the heat, and let the mixture steep for about 30 minutes to blend the flavors. Strain the seeds and herbs and discard them. Pour the flavored half-and-half into the saucepan with the reserved onion puree.

Before serving, reheat the carrot soup and stir in the remaining ⅓ cup of the half-and-half, bringing it almost to a boil. Reheat the onion mixture. In both cases, do not let the mixtures boil or they will curdle.

To serve, half fill four individual shallow soup bowls with carrot soup. In the middle of each soup bowl, carefully ladle about ¼ cup of the onion mixture.

Garnish with small carrot leaves, a sprig of lovage, or dill.

Serves 4.

# Watermelon Salad with Black Grapes and Tarragon

Most cooks use herbs in savory rather than sweet dishes such as this sophisticated fruit salad, which can be served as an appetizer or a dessert. I like to use yellow watermelon and black seedless grapes in this dish, and use only fresh tarragon, as dried has much less flavor.

2 to 2⅓ cups seeded and cubed
    yellow or red watermelon
2 cups seedless grapes, halved
½ cup white grape juice
1 teaspoon honey
1 teaspoon finely chopped fresh
    tarragon
Lemon sorbet
Garnish: small slices of watermelon
    and grapes, sprigs of tarragon

Place the watermelon and grapes into a medium-size bowl.

In a small bowl, combine the grape juice, honey, and tarragon. Pour it over the fruit and gently mix together. To serve, divide the mixture equally among four serving bowls. Top each fruit salad with a small scoop of lemon sorbet. Place the bowls on small plates and garnish with a watermelon slice, grapes, and tarragon on each plate.

Serves 4.

# Goat Cheese Cheesecake with Herbs

This is a contribution from Jesse Cool, chef and owner of the Flea Street Cafe in Menlo Park, California. Try serving it as an hors d'oeuvre with crisp apples and warm, crusty bread or homemade garlic toast. The cheese-cake must be refrigerated overnight, so plan ahead. However, it can keep for weeks.

2 pounds fresh goat cheese
1 pound cream cheese
3 eggs
2 tablespoons minced fresh rose-
    mary, oregano, or thyme, or a
    combination of all three
¾ cup finely chopped sweet red
    peppers
About 1 cup pine nuts

Preheat the oven to 375°F. Soften the goat and cream cheeses, and whip together all the ingredients except the pine nuts. Butter an 8-inch springform pan and pour in the goat cheese mixture. Spread the pine nuts evenly over the top and bake for 25 to 30 minutes. Cool to room temperature, cover, and chill the cheesecake in the refrigerator overnight. Slide a wet knife around the outside of the cheesecake to loosen it. Remove the spring and lift off the ring. Slide the cheesecake onto a plate if you choose, or simply serve it from the pan bottom. Serve at room temperature.

Serves 20 as hors d'oeuvres.

# Party Spinach Feta Strudel

This traditional flaky Greek dish has been the star at many a party. If your filo dough is frozen, defrost it overnight in the refrigerator. Remove the filo dough from the refrigerator at least 3 hours before preparing the strudel.

3 (1-pound) packages of filo
   (strudel) dough
2 pounds fresh spinach
1/3 cup salted butter
1 1/2 cups finely chopped onions
5 eggs, slightly beaten
1 pound feta cheese
1 cup chopped fresh dill
1/4 cup chopped fresh Italian
   parsley

1/4 teaspoon freshly ground black
   pepper
2 to 3 cups (4 to 6 sticks)
   unsalted butter

**To prepare the filling:**
Wash the spinach well in two or three changes of water. Put an inch of water in the bottom of a steamer and bring it to a boil. Steam half the spinach until just wilted, remove, and put in a large bowl. Repeat this procedure with the rest of the spinach. Cool the spinach and by hand squeeze out most of the liquid, then coarsely chop.

Melt the salted butter in a skillet over low heat. Add the onions and slowly cook until translucent, about 10 minutes. Add the onions to the spinach. Cool. Add the eggs, feta cheese, dill, parsley, and pepper and mix well. Chill for 30 minutes. If liquid collects, drain the mixture.

**To assemble the pastries:**
Have on hand three cookie sheets, a damp, clean dish towel, and a pastry brush. In the microwave oven, melt the unsalted butter in a small bowl. When working with filo dough, never let it dry out. Cover it with a barely damp dish towel.

Lay one sheet of filo dough on a clean surface and lightly paint a thin layer of melted butter on it. Lay another sheet on top, repeating this process until you have created four layers. Paint the top layer with butter. Cut strips approximately 3 inches wide, cutting across the width (shortest dimension) of the layered filo. Place approximately 1 1/2 teaspoons of spinach filling 1 inch in from the end of one strip. Fold a corner of the strip diagonally over the filling to form a triangle, then fold the triangle over itself all the way to the end, just as you would fold a flag. Brush it with butter and place it on a cookie sheet. (Your first few pastries will probably be uneven, but you'll soon perfect the technique.) Repeat with the remaining strips. Continue the layering procedure with the rest of the filo dough. Any leftover filling can be used to fill an omelet. (Pastries can be frozen at this point. Put them in the freezer on a cookie sheet lined with waxed paper. When they're completely frozen, transfer them to plastic freezer bags.)

Preheat the oven to 350°F. Bake for about 35 minutes, or until golden brown. Serve warm.

Makes about 60 (3-inch) pastries.

# Spinach and Fresh Oregano Pizza

**P**izza and fresh oregano are perfect partners. This is a basic pizza; chopped bell peppers, sliced tomatoes, or grilled eggplant may be substituted for some of the vegetables below. Vegetarians can omit the sausage.

    2 teaspoons olive oil
    1 small onion, minced
    1 garlic clove, minced
    ¼ pound Italian-style pork or
        turkey sausage, crumbled or
        sliced
    4 or 5 mushrooms, sliced
    3 cups fresh spinach
    Freshly ground black pepper
    1 large unbaked pizza shell
    ¼ cup feta cheese, diced
    1 to 1½ teaspoons finely chopped
        fresh oregano
    1 cup grated mozzarella cheese

Preheat oven to 450°F. In a large pan, heat the olive oil and sauté the onions, garlic, sausage, and mushrooms for about 10 minutes, or until the sausage is cooked. Add the spinach and sauté, stirring constantly, for about 1 minute, or until the spinach has wilted. Add pepper to taste. Spread the mixture on the pizza shell. Sprinkle on the feta cheese and the oregano, and top with the grated mozzarella. Bake for 10 to 15 minutes, or until the cheese has melted and the shell starts to brown.

Serves 4.

# Roast Lamb with Rosemary

Lamb with rosemary is a classic combination. Serve the lamb with roasted or mashed potatoes and spring vegetables—a classic pairing would be with fresh peas. If you are going to use ground dried rosemary, resist using the bottled version from the market, as it seldom has much flavor. Instead, take leaves of dry rosemary, put them in an electric coffee grinder, and grind your own. (Using this inexpensive appliance is well worth the flavor boost that fresh-ground seasonings give food.) Note that the lamb should marinate for at least four hours.

    1 tablespoon finely minced fresh
        rosemary or 1 teaspoon
        ground dried rosemary
    ½ cup Dijon-style mustard
    1 garlic clove, mashed to a paste
    1½ tablespoons extra-virgin olive
        oil
    1 leg of lamb (5½ to 6 pounds)

Place the rosemary, mustard, and garlic in a small bowl. Whisk in the oil a few drops at a time until all the oil has been incorporated.

To prepare the lamb, remove most of the outer layer of fat, leaving a thin layer of filament over the meat. Brush the rosemary mixture over the entire leg of lamb. Refrigerate for at least 4 hours.

Preheat the oven to 350°F. Place the lamb in a shallow roasting pan and bake for 1½ to 2 hours, or until a meat thermometer reads 145°F for medium rare. Carve the lamb into thin slices before serving.

Serves 5 to 6.

# Grilled Swordfish with Rosemary

This recipe is from Carole Saville and blends the richness of swordfish with the assertiveness of rosemary. It works equally well when broiling the swordfish instead. Note that the swordfish needs to marinate for an hour.

    ¼ cup fresh rosemary leaves and
        soft stems
    1 cup olive oil
    2 tablespoons lemon juice
    ¼ teaspoon salt
    Cayenne pepper
    4 swordfish steaks, 1 inch thick
        (about 5 ounces each)
    Garnish: 4 teaspoons finely
        chopped fresh rosemary, rose-
        mary flowers (if in bloom), and
        lemon wedges

Finely chop the rosemary. Put it in a small bowl and with the bottom of a drinking glass rub the rosemary to bruise it. In a large, deep plate, combine the olive oil, lemon juice, salt, cayenne pepper, and rosemary, stirring to combine. Rinse the swordfish and pat it dry. Turn each steak over in the marinade to coat it well. Cover and refrigerate the swordfish for 1 hour, turning it once after 30 minutes.

Grill the swordfish over a medium flame, turning it after 5 minutes. Continue to grill until the flesh is opaque when cut in the thickest part, about 5 more minutes. Remove the steaks and place on four warmed plates. Sprinkle 1 teaspoon of chopped rosemary over each serving. Further garnish with rosemary flowers and lemon wedges. Serve immediately.

Serves 4.

# Native Squash Stew

This main dish stew is a great surprise to anyone having it for the first time. As my brother-in-law in Maine says, "It's awesome," and he serves it with corn bread and a salad. My son-in-law in Los Angeles thinks it's great with warm corn tortillas. Choose a rich-flavored squash such as butternut, 'Gold Nugget,' or kaboucha; it's a perfect marriage. This stew freezes beautifully, thus the large proportions for the following recipe. You can easily change the spiciness of the dish by deleting or adding more roasted chiles or adding more hot sauce.

3 tablespoons oil

2 medium-size to large onions, chopped

9 to 10 cups winter squash, peeled and cut into 2-inch cubes

4 garlic cloves, finely chopped

1 red bell pepper, roasted, peeled, and chopped

4 to 6 fresh mild green Anaheim chiles, roasted, peeled, and chopped, or 1 or 2 small cans of mild chiles, chopped

2 or 3 ears of corn, scraped, or 1 can of niblet-style corn

2 to 3 teaspoons ground cumin

Salt and freshly ground black pepper

Hot pepper sauce

Garnish: 3 to 4 tablespoons finely chopped fresh cilantro

In a large stockpot, heat the oil and add the onions. Sauté over medium heat until translucent. Add the squash, garlic, bell pepper, chiles, corn, cumin, and 3 cups of water, cover, and simmer over low heat for 30 to 45 minutes, or until the squash is tender.

Add salt, pepper, and your favorite hot sauce to taste. Transfer the stew to a large serving bowl and sprinkle with cilantro.

Serves 8.

# Barbecued Vegetables on Rosemary Skewers

Sometimes gardener-cooks can't help themselves and have to do some "show-off" cooking. Certainly using the stout stems of upright, woody rosemaries like 'Tuscan Blue' or 'Miss Jessup's Upright' as barbecue skewers qualifies as one-upmanship cooking. You can use any recipe that requires grilling on skewers, just remember to soak the rosemary skewers and keep them away from the hottest coals.

4 strong, straight, woody stems of rosemary, ¼ inch to ⅓ inch in diameter and 10 to 14 inches long

8 to 12 large red or orange cherry tomatoes, or 2 medium paste tomatoes cut in quarters

8 to 12 boiling onions (1 to 1½ inches in diameter), peeled and parboiled for 2 minutes

1 medium-size Japanese eggplant, cut into 4 to 6 slices

1 medium-size red or yellow bell pepper, cut into approximately 12 (1-inch) pieces

1 medium-size green bell pepper, cut into approximately 12 (1-inch) pieces

**Marinade**

⅓ cup extra-virgin olive oil

1 large garlic clove, minced

2 tablespoons finely chopped fresh rosemary

Thirty minutes before you are ready to grill the vegetables, prepare the rosemary skewers and the fire. To prepare the skewers, strip the leaves off each stem by holding on to the top with one hand and grasping the stem tightly with the thumb and forefinger of your other hand and running them down the stems. Soak the stems in water for half an hour before using them. To prepare the fire, place a single layer of charcoal in your kettle grill and light it.

Divide the vegetables into four equal portions, making sure that there are vegetables of each type for each skewer. Take the rosemary skewers and thread each vegetable onto them, one at a time, alternating the different vegetables. (If the ends of the rosemary are not sharp enough to penetrate some of the vegetables, make a small hole in the vegetables with a knife.) Fill each skewer but leave an inch at the end for a handle.

To make the marinade, in a small bowl, stir together the olive oil, garlic, and rosemary. With a small brush, paint the marinade on both sides of the vegetables. Paint them again before you are ready to cook them.

When the flames have died down and the charcoal is covered with a fine gray ash, you are ready to cook your skewered vegetables. Grease the grill well and place it about 6 inches above the coals—or at the distance where you can hold your hand for about a second. Place the skewers on the grill and turn them about every 2 minutes, until they are tender and start to brown— approximately 8 minutes.

Serves 4.

# Savory Mashed Potatoes with Garden Herbs

Traditional mashed potatoes are wonderful, but adding chopped fresh herbs means infinite variations.

2 to 2½ pounds Yukon Gold or Russet-type potatoes (approximately 4 large potatoes), peeled and cut into quarters
2 garlic cloves
½ cup milk
⅓ cup heavy cream
4 tablespoons butter
1½ teaspoons finely snipped fresh chives
1 tablespoon finely chopped fresh parsley
1½ teaspoons finely chopped fresh tarragon
Dash of nutmeg
Salt and freshly ground black pepper

In a large saucepan, cover the potatoes and garlic with water and boil for 10 to 15 minutes, or until the potatoes are tender. Be careful to not overcook them. Drain off the water.

Meanwhile, in a small saucepan, heat the milk and cream. When the mixture is hot but not boiling, add the butter and continue heating until the butter has melted.

Force the potatoes and garlic through a ricer or foodmill, or mash them in a bowl with a potato masher until they are smooth. (Be careful not to overmix them, or the potatoes will get gummy.) Place the potatoes in a large saucepan and over medium heat, slowly stir in the milk mixture with a spoon until it has a creamy texture. Fold in the herbs. Add salt and pepper to taste. Serves 4.

# Stuffed Zucchini Blossoms with Goat Cheese

This elegant appetizer takes advantage of the midsummer zucchini explosion.

3 tablespoons extra-virgin olive oil, divided
1 medium onion, chopped
2 garlic cloves, minced
1 medium red bell pepper, roasted, seeded, and chopped
8 large paste tomatoes (2 pounds), peeled, seeded, and chopped
1 tablespoon tomato paste
1 teaspoon sugar
1 teaspoon balsamic vinegar
½ cup dry red wine
½ teaspoon chopped fresh thyme
¼ cup fresh basil, chopped
Salt and freshly ground black pepper to taste
8 small zucchini with their blossoms
6 ounces creamy-style goat cheese
2 tablespoons fresh basil, chopped
Garnish: fresh thyme leaves or chopped basil

Start by preparing the sauce. In a large saucepan heat 2 tablespoons of the olive oil and sauté the onions over medium heat until tender, about 7 minutes. Add the garlic and sauté 4 minutes, or until they are soft but not brown. Add the bell pepper, tomatoes, tomato paste, sugar, and balsamic vinegar and simmer over low heat for about 45 minutes, or until the sauce is fairly thick, stirring occasionally. Add the wine, thyme, and basil and cook the sauce for 10 more minutes over medium heat. Press the sauce through a coarse sieve. You should have approximately 2 cups of sauce. Return the sauce to the saucepan, season it with salt and pepper, and set it aside.

Preheat the oven to 350°F. Carefully examine the zucchini blossoms for insects and remove the stamens and pistils. In a small bowl blend the goat cheese with the basil. Fill each blossom with a scant tablespoon of the cheese. Try not to overstuff the blossoms or the cheese will ooze out as it cooks. Brush the bottom of a baking dish with 1 teaspoon of olive oil. Place the zucchini into the dish and drizzle them with the remaining olive oil. Bake them for 15 to 20 minutes, or until they are al dente and starting to brown, and the cheese has melted.

Warm the sauce and divide it equally among the plates. Spread the sauce to create a small pool on each plate and place the stuffed zucchini in the middle of the sauce. Garnish with the herbs and serve.

Serves 8 as an appetizer, 4 as a side dish.

# Fennel Rice with Pistachios

This "fragrantly" flavorful dish makes a wonderful accompaniment for fish or roasted chicken, or you can add grated cheese before you cover the rice with the bread-crumb mixture for a vegetarian main course. I prefer to use Carolina or Basmati rice as they have a light, rich texture.

2 cups uncooked white long-grain rice,

4½ cups vegetable broth, divided

1 bay leaf

2 Florence fennel bulbs (3 to 4 inches wide) with greens (approximately 2 pounds)

2 tablespoons olive oil

1 large onion, coarsely chopped

2 garlic cloves, minced

1 teaspoon fennel seeds

1 teaspoon coriander seeds

2 tablespoons chopped fresh parsley

Salt and freshly ground black pepper to taste

1 cup grated Gruyère cheese (optional)

1½ cups fresh bread crumbs

⅓ cup chopped shelled pistachio nuts or shelled almonds

⅛ teaspoon freshly ground black pepper, plus extra

1 tablespoon butter, melted

Place the rice in a large saucepan or rice cooker. Add 3½ cups of the vegetable broth and the bay leaf. Bring it to a boil, then cover and cook over low heat for about 20 minutes, or until the rice is tender and the liquid has been absorbed. Remove the bay leaf.

Meanwhile, remove the fennel leaves from the stems, setting aside a few leaves for a garnish. Finely chop the leaves. Cut the fennel bulbs crosswise into fine dice.

In a large frying pan, heat the olive oil over medium heat. Add the onions, garlic, and diced fennel bulbs and sauté, stirring occasionally, for about 10 minutes, or until translucent.

With a blender or mortar and pestle, coarsely grind the fennel seeds and coriander seeds.

In a large bowl, combine the onion mixture, cooked rice, chopped fennel greens, parsley, and the ground coriander and fennel seeds. Add salt and pepper to taste. (At this point you could stir in the nuts and serve immediately as a simple side dish.)

Preheat the oven to 350°F. Grease a 3-quart shallow ovenproof casserole dish. Add remaining vegetable broth to the rice and mix. Spread the rice mixture evenly in the dish. Sprinkle grated Gruyère cheese over the rice, if desired. In a small bowl, combine the bread crumbs, nuts, and the ⅛ teaspoon of black pepper. Sprinkle the bread crumbs over the rice. Drizzle melted butter on top. Bake for about 15 minutes, or until the top is a light golden brown. Serve garnished with fennel leaves.

Serves 6.

# Leeks and New Potatoes with Savory Cream

The herb savory brings out the richness of the vegetables. Nowhere is it more evident than in this voluptuous dish in which it flavors leeks, cream, and potatoes.

1 pint whipping cream

4 (3-inch) sprigs of fresh winter savory, divided

14 to 16 new potatoes (2 to 2½ inches in diameter), washed but not peeled

1 teaspoon salt

10 to 12 young leeks, ½ inch to 1 inch in diameter, or 4 large leeks

1 tablespoon butter

¼ teaspoon nutmeg

Salt and freshly ground black pepper

Garnish: fresh sprigs of winter savory

Put the cream and 3 sprigs of the savory in a saucepan and bring it to a boil. Remove from the heat and let the cream steep for about 1 hour.

In another saucepan, boil the potatoes in water with salt and the remaining sprig of savory until just tender, approximately 20 minutes.

Clean the leeks by partially cutting them lengthwise and flushing them with water. Cut the white parts diagonally in pieces approximately 2 inches long. (For large leeks, cut into 1-inch pieces.) If the lower portions of the green leaves are tender, slice them as

well. (Use tough green tops to make stock.) Sauté the leeks in butter for 5 minutes, or until tender, and set aside.

Remove the savory sprigs from the cream and discard. Bring the cream to a boil and reduce until about half remains, approximately 6 to 10 minutes. Season with nutmeg, salt, and pepper.

To serve, reheat leeks if necessary. Arrange the leeks on part of a serving plate. Drain the potatoes and place them on the other side of the plate. Pour the reduced cream over the leeks and potatoes and garnish with savory sprigs.

Serves 4 as a side dish.

# Carrots and Apricots with Fresh Chervil

Carole Saville and I have written an herb series for *Country Living Gardener* for many years and when I asked her what chervil recipes were her favorites, she gave me this one. You'll see that apricots and chervil add a sprightly note to steamed carrots.

    ¼ cup slivered dried apricots
    1 pound carrots
    2 tablespoons walnut oil
    2 tablespoons fresh squeezed
        orange juice
    Salt and freshly ground black pepper
    ½ teaspoon anise seeds
    2 tablespoons minced fresh chervil

In a small bowl, cover the apricots with hot water and set them aside to plump for 30 minutes. Peel the carrots and cut them into thin slices. Steam the carrots for 5 to 10 minutes, or until they're tender but not soft. Remove them from the steamer basket and discard the water, then return them to the warm pot. Drain the apricots and add them to the carrots. Stir in the walnut oil, orange juice, salt, and pepper to taste, and cover the pot. Heat the anise seeds in a small, dry cast-iron skillet, stirring constantly just until they perfume the air, about 1 minute. Add the anise seeds and chervil to the carrots. Stir to combine. Serve immediately.

Serves 4.

# Golden Beets with Dill Vinaigrette

Golden beets are startlingly beautiful; paired with dill, they taste sweet, rich, and earthy.

> 6 medium-size golden beets
> ⅓ cup olive oil
> 3 tablespoons white wine vinegar
> 1 teaspoon minced fresh dill
> Salt and freshly ground black
>     pepper
> 1 large head of butter lettuce,
>     leaves washed and separated
> Garnish: purple pansies or nastur-
>     tiums

Wash the beets and steam them for approximately 40 minutes, or until just tender. Peel and slice them. While they are still warm, make the vinaigrette.

In a bowl, stir the oil, vinegar, and dill. Pour the vinaigrette over the beets and gently stir; let the beets sit for an hour at room temperature to absorb some of the flavors, stirring them occasionally. Refrigerate. On a large platter, arrange lettuce leaves, top them with the beets, and garnish with flowers.

Serves 4.

# edible flower gardens

It's incredible how many flowers or parts of flowers I've eaten in the past few years—lavender petals made into ice cream, zucchini blossoms stuffed with ricotta cheese, roses used in butter, to name just a few. And I've made an effort to share the experience, serving unsuspecting guests unadorned pineapple guava petals and an Art Deco–style cake with candied pansies. Not only do I eat edible flowers, but I've become a missionary in promoting them!

I'd love to be able to tell you about the first flower I ever ate, but I can't remember what it was. It was probably a nasturtium, though, eaten nearly twenty years ago. I'm certain I started slowly, since to eat flowers seemed odd

to me, maybe even taboo. I remember eating rice garnished with calendula petals in Vermont and thinking that they made the dish colorful but didn't add much to the flavor. Later, I tried a

few pansy petals served in a restaurant salad and still wasn't won over. It wasn't until I tasted lavender ice cream at an herb seminar that I became really enthusiastic. It was fantastic! I determined there and then to learn more about edible flowers.

Since that time, I've probably asked everyone I know to eat flowers. A few people just plunge right in with delight, as if I've given them permission to enjoy a new pleasure. But most people are much more hesitant. One friend would accept my dinner invitation only after warning, "But I won't try any of your darn flowers!" You'd have thought I was offering her fried caterpillars. I've tried to get people to explain their hesitation about eating flowers, but they seem to have a hard time doing so. I certainly have difficulty explaining my initial reluctance. Why do others? Is it because we hesitate to try any new food? Somewhat. Is it a concern about the safety of eating them?

---

Edible flowers can be tucked into almost any garden scene. Here (*left*), pansies, roses, and chrysanthemums grow in my back garden. A bouquet of edible flowers (*above*) includes calendulas, scarlet runner beans, lavender, nasturtiums, and chive blossoms. The photo spread on pages 2 and 3 shows a sunny border designed for a client. I interspersed the edible roses, nasturtiums, and marigolds among the nonedible lantanas and plumbagos. I used their blue and lavender blooms to tone down the fiery reds and oranges.

Maybe. But I've just about concluded that, mainly, people believe that flowers are almost magical, so beautiful that only the eyes should feast on them. To those folks, eating flowers seems a bit greedy.

I've read everything I could find about edible flowers. I've asked every chef I've interviewed about his or her experiences with them. And I've tasted every edible flower I could get my hands on, even stooping on occasion to sneak a bite of my hostess' centerpiece.

I've found the information available on edible flowers to be a strange hodgepodge. Much of our knowledge about edible flowers comes from old herbals. But when I turned to the herbals themselves, my confusion mounted. Eating flowers was commonplace in medieval Europe, when food often had a medicinal as well as a nutritional purpose. Sometimes the old recipes included dangerous flowers. Thus, a dish might call for two or three blossoms of foxglove, which is classified as poisonous today. True, we use foxglove to make digitalis, a heart stimulant, but only in carefully measured doses. I realized, as I read the old recipes, that the term *poisonous* is relative.

Displays of edible flowers (*right*) at farmer's markets and exhibitions such as this one at the Tasting of Summer Produce in Oakland, California, get more sophisticated every year. On display are fuchsias, Johnny-jump-ups, tuberous begonias, nasturtiums, and rose petals. Flower-petal confetti (*far right*) is a versatile little pleasure. Prior to serving, it can be sprinkled over an entree plate, a salad, or pastries.

As if the herbals' folk-medicine approach didn't make it difficult enough to determine which flowers are safe to eat, our forebearers often called flowers by different names. For instance, what we know as calendula they called marigold; what we call cottage pink was gillyflower. So I was faced with the challenge of making sure the flowers referred to in the recipes matched the flowers we grow today.

And then which of the edible flowers are palatable? I collected a number of modern lists of edible flowers and cautiously began my taste testing. Some were absolutely horrible! Obviously, no one had tasted them before adding them to the lists. For example, some marigolds have a slightly lemony taste, others are tasteless, but the taste of most falls somewhere between skunk and quinine. Furthermore, none of these lists gave much guidance on

*how* to eat the different kinds of flowers. I remember innocently putting an entire mullein petal into my mouth and finding it to be horribly astringent. I had the same experience with a carnation petal. Later, I learned that you need to first remove the terrible-tasting white part at the base of the petals.

Flowers should become a perma-nent part of our cuisine. They offer another alternative to salt and sugar as seasonings. Not only do flowers make interesting seasonings, especially for those fruits and vegetables we want to increase in our diets, but their aesthetic value as decoration is obvious.

In researching this book, I asked every gardener, chef, and food expert I could talk to how they prepared edible flowers. And I arranged for a few edible flower gardens to be grown for this project: one by Carole Saville, an herb specialist in Los Angeles; another by the folks at the Chez Panisse restau-rant in Berkeley, California; not to mention my own little edible flower gardens.

This harvest of edible flowers (*left*) is held by Judy Dornstroek. She and her husband grow edible flowers in their Pennsylvania greenhouse to sell to restaurants. Included are pink rose-scented geraniums, borage flowers, and nasturtiums of many colors. A harvest from my garden (*below, top*) includes broccoli and mustard blossoms, violas, violets, Johnny-jump-ups, the tiny maché flowers, calendulas, and nasturtiums. Edible flowers also can be used in bouquets. Here is a striking orange and blue bouquet from my garden (*below, bottom*) with lots of nasturtiums and the nonedible bachelor buttons.

If you're still hesitant about jumping in and growing an edible flower garden, I urge you to read along for inspiration. I bet that by the time you finish the cooking section, the sheer anticipation of working with flowers in your kitchen will have you planning your own edible flower garden.

Edible flowers can be found in all sorts of landscape situations. Chestnut roses (*left*) grace a front yard in Jackson, Mississippi. Nasturtiums (*above, top*) cascade out of a planter and complement the Spanish architecture in a California garden. In New Jersey, many varieties of scented geraniums (*above, bottom*) line a walk at Well-Sweep Herb Farm.

# how to grow edible flowers

All sorts of plants produce edible flowers, but it's the annual flowers—those that are seeded, grown, and produced all in just one season, like nasturtiums, pansies, and squash blossoms—that people are most familiar with. The easiest way to obtain edible flowers is to inventory the plants already growing in your garden.

First, peruse the "Encyclopedia of Edible Flowers" (page 123) to see which plants produce edible flowers; then walk around your property to see which ones you have. Be sure to check out your vegetable garden too, as some of those plants produce great flowers. Then, before you go any further, get acquainted with the accompanying poisonous plant list (pages 108-109). To make sure you properly identify the flowers, please obtain a couple of basic field guides to edible plants (see the Bibliography, page 199). And just to be safe, you might take a sample of whatever you are considering eating to a local nursery for a positive identification.

Once you have inventoried your landscape for flowering delicacies, consider adding a few choice perennials, bulbs, shrubs, or trees. Daylilies, tulips, roses, and apple blossoms, for example, all have edible flowers. Because they grow for years—perennially—such plants need a permanent site; consider carefully where to locate them.

Perennials are generally planted from divisions or from grafted plant material, depending on the species, and they need good soil preparation and drainage, though they are usually not as fussy about soil fertility and mois-

My back-patio edible flower garden (*right*) was designed with pink in mind. The flowers are a combination of annuals and perennials. A miniature pink rose sits in a container, and the perennial Alpine strawberries, English daisies, pinks, and daylilies fill in most of the bed. I supplement the beds with pansies in the spring and chrysanthemums in the fall.

ture as annual flowers and vegetables are. For more information on planting perennials, see Appendix A, "Planting and Maintenance" (page 184).

Most of the plants that produce edible flowers need at least six hours of sun each day. Add perennial, edible flowers to your landscape easily by installing a border of lavender plants along a driveway; putting in a small sitting area surrounded by daylilies and chrysanthemums; adding a little herb corner off the patio planted with sage, chives, fennel, and bee balm; or

Carole Saville (*top*) helps plant my nasturtium garden. One year, I planted a whole garden of nasturtiums (*below*) and tested a dozen varieties. Here, Adam Lane and Jody Main harvest handfuls of blooms from that garden. The nasturtiums all tasted the same, but the color variations were fantastic.

All herb flowers (*above*) are edible. Consequently, an herb garden is a great place to find more flowers for your salad. Here, my street-side herb border contains nepitella (Italian mint), lavender, and lemon thyme, all herbs that produce flowers. Not all herbs bloom, however. Included in the bed are variegated oregano and sage, which never produce flowers. For a larger selection of edible flowers, I added blue and yellow violas and pansies to the herb planting.

planting more than your usual number of tulips in the fall. If you're feeling a little more ambitious, plant a redbud or apple tree to give you privacy from a neighbor's window. Maybe you've always wanted a lilac; now you have one more excuse to plant one. By adding just a few plants here and there, you can add quite a bit to your repertoire in the kitchen.

The "Encyclopedia of Edible Flowers" (page 123) details which varieties produce the best edible flowers and provides information on growing all the plants mentioned—enough to get you started and give you an idea of how much care the plants need. Occasionally you may need to consult other books for different information—local cultivars or conditions, for example. Be aware that the authors of most of the flower-culture books in this country do not anticipate your eating the flowers and therefore occasionally recommend pesticides that are unsafe for human consumption. (Nontoxic, organic pest and disease controls are given in Appendix B, "Pest and Disease Control," page 192.)

Unlike vegetable varieties, the flowers bred at nurseries have been selected not for their flavor but for their appearance and growing ease. Therefore,

taste as many varieties as possible before you plant. Visit the gardens of friends and neighbors and taste a few flowers at a time. *But beware of poisons!* Before you start tasting flowers, let alone planning your garden, you need a brief lesson on poisonous plants.

## Poisonous Plants

What is poisonous, anyway? When I began my research I was naive enough to assume that I would be able to find a definitive list of poisonous flowering plants. No such luck. There are plenty of lists of poisonous plants, but none that completely resolves the issue of what is and is not poisonous. I had to do my own legwork, so I began at the beginning, with *Webster's Third: poison:* "A substance . . . that in suitable quantities has properties harmful or fatal to an organism when it is brought into contact with or absorbed by the organism."

So the two crucial factors are chemical contents and dosage. As to the former, plants containing alkaloids, glycosides, resins, alcohols, phenols, and oxalates are potentially poisonous, but their toxicity depends on the amount of these substances they contain. After all, many poisonous plants are also valuable medicines; it is the dosage that determines whether the end product is medicinal or toxic. In fact, some poisonous-plant lists actually include spinach and chard because they contain oxalic acid, which is poisonous in large quantities.

Still, determining how much of a substance makes a plant or serving toxic is a matter for chemists. Obviously, the more you ingest—eating foxglove ice cream rather than just a single petal on a salad plate—the greater the hazard. My advice and the rule I follow is: don't take chances. If a flowering plant is on *any* list of poisonous plants, I don't eat it—not even a single petal—until I have more information. And if I can't find the plant on any list of *edible* or poisonous plants, I assume it is *not* edible.

Here are some guidelines I have gathered from food technologists and environmental botanists:

1. Positively identify the plant—Latin name and all. As with mushrooms, identification is crucial.

2. Birds and animals are unharmed by some plants that are poisonous to humans. The gray squirrel can safely eat the deadly amanita mushroom, and birds regularly gorge on the irritating red elderberry berries. So don't depend on guinea pigs of any species to guide you.

3. Not all parts of toxic plants are necessarily poisonous. For instance, rhubarb stalks and potatoes are edible, but the leaves of both plants are poisonous.

4. Some plants, such as pokeweed, are poisonous only at certain times of the year.

5. Because individuals can be allergic to substances that are not generally poisonous—wheat and milk, for example—when you first taste a new food, eat only a small amount.

6. Just because most members of a particular plant family are not poisonous does not mean that all are.

7. Heating or cooking in water removes many toxins, but not all.

8. Never use any flower as a garnish if it's not edible. In this day and age, when diners eat flowers, you're just asking for an accidental poisoning.

9. Make sure it's clear to children that some flowers are edible and others can make them sick.

10. And a most important point: You can cause damage and not even know it. Because a plant does not make you sick to your stomach or cause your heart to race or make you break out in a rash doesn't mean that it's safe. Some toxic reactions take time to manifest them-

selves; others will never be detected. For example, some plants contain chemicals that cause cancer, abortions, or birth defects; others are filled with chemicals that raise your blood pressure, rob the body of calcium, or tie up iron.

Below is a list of a few of the most common poisonous plants and the parts of the plants known to be dangerous.

Amaryllis *Hippeastrum puniceum*: Bulb
Anemone *Anemone tuberosa* and other
    spp.: All
Autumn Crocus *Colchicum autumnale*:
    All

Azalea *Rhododendron* spp.: All

Belladonna Lily (Naked Lady)
   *Amaryllis belladonna*: Bulb

Bird-of-Paradise *Strelitzia reginae*:
   Seeds and pods

Buckeye (Horse Chestnut) *Aesculus
   arguta* and *A. hippocastanum* and
   other spp.: Seeds, flowers, and leaves

Buttercup *Ranunculus* spp.: All

Caladium *Caladium bicolor* and other
   spp.: All

Cardinal Flower *Lobelia cardinalis*:
   Particularly the bulb

Clematis *Clematis*: All

Daffodil *Narcissus pseudonarcissus*:
   Particularly the bulb

Datura *Datura meteloides*: All

Delphinium *Delphinium* spp.: All

Foxglove *Digitalis purpurea*: All

Gloriosa Lily *Gloriosa* spp.: All

Hydrangea *Hydrangea* spp.: All

Iris *Iris* spp.: Leaves and rootstock

Jessamine *Gelsemium sempervirens*: All

Lantana *Lantana* spp.: All

Larkspur *Delphinium* spp.: All

Lily-of-the-Valley *Convallaria majalis*:
   All

Lupine *Lupinus* spp.: All

Monkshood *Aconitum* spp.: All

Narcissus *Narcissus* spp.: All

Oleander *Nerium oleander*: All

Poinsettia *Euphorbia pulcherrima*: All

Most landscapes contain both edible and nonedible flowers. It's important for children in particular to be taught the difference. Here, edible roses, society garlic, and nasturtiums grow among the nonedible coreopsis and iris.

Rhododendron *Rhododendron* spp.: All

Star-of-Bethlehem *Ornithogalum* spp.:
   All

Sweet Pea *Lathyrus* spp.: All

Tansy *Tanacetum vulgare*: All

Wisteria *Wisteria floribunda* and *W.
   sinensis*: Pods and seeds

# my edible flower gardens

My front walk (*right*) is festooned with edible flowers, including roses, winter savory, society garlic, the species marigolds 'Lemon Gem,' and 'Empress of India' nasturtiums.

I always have edible flowers growing in my yard. Some (lavender, daylilies, and anise hyssop) grow in ornamental flower borders, others (rosemary and thyme) are part of my herb corner, and still others (squash and broccoli) grow in the vegetable garden. Sometimes, though, just for fun I like to try new edible flower varieties or illustrate how little room it takes to grow a selection of flowers for the kitchen, so I grow tiny gardens of only edible flowers.

It never stops amazing me how little space it takes to grow an enormous number and variety of blossoms for the table. The garden illustrated on pages 18–19 was located in my front-yard vegetable garden and included eleven species of edible flowers—enough to make a huge impact in the kitchen. I chose yellow, orange, and blue flowers. The total area of this little flower garden was six feet by twelve feet with a two-foot-wide path running through the middle, or about sixty square feet of bed space. As it turned out, half that size would have been plenty.

I live in a mild-winter area, so I planted my garden in early fall. Gardeners in USDA Zones 1 through 8 would plant this type of garden in the spring, starting many of the plants in flats six weeks before the average last-frost date. I planted the mizuna, arugula, nasturtiums, and calendulas directly in the garden from seeds. The rest of the plants came from a nursery.

My soil is in enviable condition after twenty years of soil building, so I didn't need to add amendments at planting time. First, I laid out the beds. Because they are the tallest, I filled the back

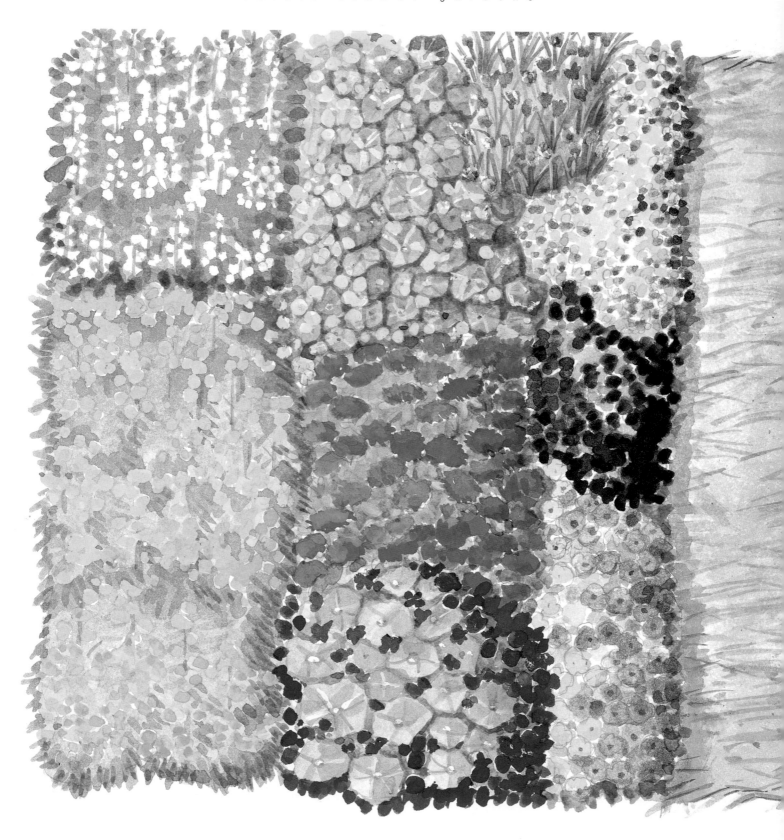

One year, I took the middle two beds out of my vegetable garden and planted them primarily with annual edible flowers. In spring, these little plots produced enough flowers to decorate a panoply of fancy platters. The drawing (*above*) indicates the location of the plants. In the back row, the north side of the garden (*to the left*), I planted the tallest plants so they would not shade the shorter species. The back row contains (*top to bottom*) arugula and mizuna (a Japanese mustard). The next row contains yellow nasturtiums and a chive plant, orange calendulas, and red

and orange nasturtiums. The front row contains yellow and lavender violas and 'Antique' mix pansies. Across the path (*top to bottom*), are romaine lettuces, yellow violas, white English daisies, Alpine strawberries, and the red lettuce 'Lolla Rossa.' In the middle is a cluster of tulips, and the front row was planted with bunching onions, purple violas, and more English daisies.

My little annual edible flower garden (*left*) in early spring produced tulips, violas, mustard flowers, and a few English daisies. A few weeks later, the same garden was in full swing (*above*) and the violas and nasturtiums were exuberant, growing in among each other, as were the chives, pansies, and calendulas.

row of one bed with arugula and mizuna, a Japanese-type mustard. The middle row contained nasturtiums and calendulas, which grow to about eighteen inches. In the front row, I planted the shorter pansies, violas, Johnny-jump-ups, and chives. In another bed, I included strawberries, pansies, English daisies, and tulips as well as half a dozen heads of romaine and frilly red lettuces and a cluster of bunching onions—all great for salads. I could have included cilantro, fennel, radishes, bush peas, broccoli, and many more types of mustard, but I planted them in the vegetable garden that year because I like to rotate crops.

Over the years I have noticed that the cool-weather edible flowers are the savory ones that are great for salads, appetizers, and garnishes for winter and spring meals. The sweet flowers on roses, lavender, honeysuckle, and scented geraniums all bloom in warm weather. That winter, I was able to harvest pansies, violas, Johnny-jump-ups, and calendulas—all great for salads and garnishes—from early winter through late spring. The frost knocked out my nasturtiums, so I replanted them in early spring. Soon, the tulips, English daisies, mizuna, and the arugula came into their glory. I could now make an even greater range of appetizers and butters and fancier salads. In the middle of spring, the nasturtiums kicked in and the strawberries started to flower (and

kept going through the summer). In late spring the chives came into bloom, the English daisies were starting to dwindle, and the mizuna went to seed and were pulled out. A few weeks later I needed to pull out most of the plants in order to plant summer vegetables. If I had the space to allow most of the edible flower plants to go to seed (as I do some years), the nasturtiums, arugula, Johnny-jump-ups, calendulas, and mizuna would have reseeded themselves and the next fall very little planting would have been needed to renew the beds (the strawberries, chives, and English daisies are perennials).

I planted another edible flower garden off my back patio (see page 105). It had a completely different color scheme: burgundy pansies, pink dianthus, light yellow 'Stella de Oro' dwarf daylilies, primrose yellow nasturtiums, Alpine strawberries, baby-pink roses, and variegated society garlic. Probably the most dramatic and fun edible flower garden I ever created was one planted with only nasturtiums—ten different varieties, to be exact (see page 106). It was eye-opening to see how many different varieties there were. Some were double, others were bicolored, and still others had green and white foliage. Of course, it produced a "gazillion" nasturtiums, and everyone who visited left with a big enough bouquet to cook with for a week.

Many edible flowers will reseed themselves like crazy. This little corner of my garden (below) grows by itself. Every spring it is completely filled with Johnny-jump-ups, nasturtiums, mâche, and watercress with its edible lacy white blossoms shown on the right.

## The Chez Panisse
## Flower Garden

A number of years ago, I invited Andrea Crawford, then manager of the Chez Panisse restaurant garden in Berkeley, California, to join me in an experiment: growing a prototypical edible flower garden with which the chefs could experiment. She and Alice Waters, the executive chef of Chez Panisse, had been growing and serving edible flowers for years and were eager to learn even more. In this garden we grew flowers that none of us had ever used in the kitchen before.

To begin, we looked over my list of edible flowers, perused seed catalogs for unusual varieties, and ordered a good selection. Both Andrea and I gathered information from everyone we knew who had grown our selections. Jan Blüm, of Seeds Blüm, sent us 'Fragrance' dianthus seeds; Renee Shepherd, of Renee's Garden, sent us 'Kablouna' calendula, anise hyssop, and 'Whirlybird' nasturtium seeds; and we both raided our own supplies of seeds and plants. We concentrated mainly on annual flowers because we wanted to evaluate the flowers in the kitchen within a year and because they are easiest for most gardeners to obtain. Andrea had been producing borage, Johnny-jump-ups, lavender, climbing nasturtiums, violas, mustard, radishes, chicory, scented geraniums, and herbs for the restaurant, and she chose varieties from among her favorites. For years, I had been growing scarlet runner beans, English daisies, and marigolds, but I had never tasted their flowers and was curious about them, so I chose the most promising varieties. I also selected 'Empress of India' and 'Alaska' nasturtiums, two particular varieties I had never used in the kitchen.

Summertime temperatures in Berkeley are moderated by morning fog, and few days exceed 90°F. The winters are mild, with temperatures seldom dropping below freezing. Though you might be hesitant at first about trying to duplicate much of this garden if you live in a northern region, almost all the flowers can actually be grown equally well anywhere in the country. The soil in the Berkeley garden was clay with a tremendous amount of organic matter added. The beds were in wonderful shape after years of loving care. Andrea, like most good gardeners, is passionate about soil preparation, and her years of effort

Andrea Crawford (*left*) and Alice Waters compare notes on the edible flowers growing in the Chez Panisse garden. A harvest of edible flowers (*right*) from the Chez Panisse garden includes hollyhocks, squash blossom, nasturtiums, 'Lemon Gem' marigolds, calendulas, runner beans, and gladiolas.

Nasturtiums and daylilies frame a garden bench.

showed. Her garden received no rain from May through September, and summer watering was a constant necessity.

Andrea and I sat down to discuss both her experiences in the garden and the chefs' experiences in the kitchen. She was eager to sum it all up. She reminded me that she and Alice had been planning a pansy garden for the restaurant and had already planted flats. It had seemed natural to add hollyhocks, scarlet runner beans, anise hyssop, 'Austrian Copper' roses, 'Adnami' chrysanthemums, Alpine strawberries, and 'Lemon Gem' marigolds and to make the new, expanded garden both an ornamental

border and a productive garden. We agreed to try to grow the approximate amounts a home gardener would use. "Well," said Andrea, "we planted far more than a person could ever use at home. In fact, that narrow strip, which is thirty feet by two and a half feet, produced more than the restaurant could use; but we viewed the beds as an ornamental garden that a person could also eat out of, and that was really very nice."

Andrea reported that Stokes Seeds had the best selection and that she could get just about all the varieties she needed from them. Thompson & Morgan, on the other hand, turned out to be really frustrating. They offered a

large number of varieties, but Andrea found that they often seemed to be out of what she wanted and sent back credit slips instead of seeds.

In the end, the most successful and versatile edible flowers were the species Andrea had always grown for the restaurant—the nasturtiums, borage, and calendulas. Of the new flowers planted, the pansies—all varieties—were probably the most useful and were a lot of fun as well. The chefs used them as garnishes and chopped them into butters. The anise hyssop was very flavorful. The runner blossoms were tasty too—the chefs mixed them with other flowers and put them in salads. "Of the nasturtiums," Andrea told me, "we liked 'Alaska' and 'Empress of India.' The flowers of these varieties are similar to those of most other varieties, but the leaves are beautiful, and when they are small they are quite delicious. We hadn't used those before. With nasturtiums, taste is the most important factor, and that's affected by how you grow them. If you start them without much water, they're quite hot to the taste. They grow best in really lush conditions, and then they're much milder."

On the other hand, the hollyhocks were a complete failure—they didn't have much flavor and had a slippery quality like that of okra. Still, Andrea thought they might be good dipped in batter and fried tempura-style. She went on to say, "Most of the calendulas we tried didn't impress me as much as our simple pot marigolds, which self-seed right here in the garden. They have large flowers and nothing seems to affect them. I don't like 'Kablouna,' because you can't get the petals off the tight head easily. And I found Stokes' claims about their calendulas—all these so-called scarlet, gold, and apricot tones—to be an overstatement. The differences among them are very subtle."

Andrea told me they did a lot of experimenting with the flowers in the kitchen. For example, she picked two deep tubs—that's probably about ten gallons—of nasturtium flowers. She then asked the chefs to get creative with them, and they made a soup with potatoes and the nasturtiums. According to Andrea, it was a total flop. "It was really awful," she said. "It had kind of a slimy texture. So we found out that you can't use nasturtiums in great quantities; they have to be used quite sparingly." Their most successful way of using nasturtiums was to chop them and mash the bits into butter. The butter then looks like it has been laced with confetti, especially when borage and pansies are chopped up along with the nasturtiums, to get blue and purple. "It's very pretty," said Andrea, "and you can put it on pasta, steak, or toast. Alice [Waters] also found this to be a good way to use flowers that have started to wilt. Squash blossoms, too, are wonderful. The chefs stuff them with cheese, or chop and fry them and serve them over pasta. They also sauté them with vegetables. Squash blossoms are very versatile and have a pleasant, delicate flavor."

Chez Panisse chefs use flowers not only in salads and butter but in many of their famous desserts. They put fresh flowers on cakes and soufflés or candy them and use them whole or chopped. The sugar makes the flowers sparkle. "Very pretty on a chocolate cake," Andrea said. "The chefs sprinkle it on the sides and then, using a small doily as a stencil over the top, make a little design all the way around of sparkling, multicolored glitter. This glitter idea came from using the delicate candied flowers. It turned out to be a great way to use the broken ones."

The chefs love to use the flowers as flavorings in ice cream. Before making the basic custard mix, they steep the petals in milk for as long as it takes to flavor it—anywhere from a few hours to a day, depending on the intensity they want. Then they strain out the flowers. They aim to flavor the custard slightly stronger than they want the end result, because some of the flavor gets lost during freezing. The most successful flower ice cream, and Andrea's personal favorite, is anise hyssop, but the chefs have made ice cream with everything from rose petals, lavender, and almond blossoms to many of the scented geraniums.

"Over the years," Andrea concluded, "we've found that you really have to think about how you use flowers. They should enhance the meal, not just be thrown randomly onto the plate or into the salad. The flower garnishes, for instance, need to have some relation to the food. So thyme flowers in a savory soup or chive blossoms in a salad instead of onion would be great, but just floating pansies by themselves on a soup doesn't make any sense.

"I would definitely grow all the edible flowers again, even the hollyhocks. They're so beautiful, and it's fun to share them with your friends. And there may be ways to use them that I just haven't discovered. I think having a flower border that's entirely edible is a good enough reason in itself to plant it. People who visit the restaurant are delighted with the edible flowers. All in all, it seems a great way to combine the beautiful flowers in the garden with what you enjoy on your table."

# Alice Waters

Alice Waters is the proprietor and inspiration behind one of this country's most famous and revolutionary restaurants, Chez Panisse, in Berkeley, California. Although I had worked with Alice casually over the years, I never appreciated her vast range of talent and knowledge until I interviewed her specifically about edible flowers. While other chefs can talk about *some* of the most common edible flowers, Alice expounds on *many* with an excitement that's infectious.

"How do patrons react to flowers on their plate?" I asked. "The flowers are a fascination," Alice said. "People really focus on them and are very curious. Some people refuse to eat them, but about half will taste them readily. I like to serve them in such a way that they're tasty and accessible to people; a large flower by itself is a little intimidating. I like to incorporate Johnny-jump-ups or nasturtium petals in salads—or serve them in ice cream or butter."

I gave Alice the list of edible flowers I had compiled and asked her to comment on those she had

tried. Her face brightened as she perused the list; she seemed to be able to replay the tastes and feelings of those she had used.

"Calendulas have a real nice flavor," she began. "Not too strong, but kind of peppery—even a little grassy. I use fresh petals in salads, or I like to dry them and use them in soups in the winter. Honeysuckle is good too," she continued. "It's very sweet and tastes just like it smells; it's quite extraordinary in some desserts. You don't need much of it, though, just a little spoonful.

Alice Waters is proprietor of Chez Panisse Restaurant in Berkeley and one of the most influential chefs in the world of fresh produce.

and flavors seem suspended.

"And certainly we have to talk about roses and violets. Rose petals are fantastic; they have all different flavors, depending on the variety. On one special occasion I used 'Damask' roses in ice cream and garnished it with deep red-orange 'Joseph's Coat' rose petals that had been dipped in egg white and sprinkled with sugar. Another time I chopped candied rose petals so they looked like little sparklies—very special. I find brightly colored varieties

"Lavender is wonderful. You can use it in both sweet and savory dishes, as a marinade for meats, or for lavender ice cream. I'm crazy about nasturtiums too. 'Empress of India,' which has a dark-red color, has a spicy, peppery flavor. I enjoy using the 'Alaska' variety in salads because the foliage is so beautiful—variegated green and white. I also use nasturtiums to top soups, salads, or pizzas—for example, smoked salmon pizza. Just put them on top at the last minute so they won't wilt. In butters, the colors

most effective. And we use fragrant violets in late winter; we candy them and then use them to garnish sherbets, or we fold fresh violets into ice cream just before we serve it."

The day I interviewed Alice, a gentleman from Texas called to find out if Chez Panisse was the restaurant that served edible flowers; he wanted to come try some. It seems that people are finding delight in trying new tastes, and Chez Panisse leads the way.

# encyclopedia of edible flowers

The following entries detail what I consider the most versatile edible flowers. The basic cultural information on preparing the soil, planting, seed starting, watering, mulching, fertilizing, pruning, and controlling pests and diseases is covered in Appendices A and B (pages 184-195).

You may notice that a few species occasionally sold as "edible" flowers—bachelor's buttons, impatiens, and snapdragons—are not listed. There is no evidence in any of the historical or scientific literature to indicate that they are edible. Why then are they regarded as edible? I've been able to trace it all back to an article published in the late

1980s by a very reputable magazine. Upon calling the editor to see where the author had obtained this information, I was shocked to learn that the list came from a young grower who "thought," but had no proof, that these

plants were edible. Two other flowers on that infamous list are stock and petunias. Although stock was eaten during famine in southern Europe, the question remains: why didn't people eat stock at other times? Does it taste bad or does it have long-term side effects? According to Craig Dremann of the Redwood City Seed Company, the Andean Indians used petunias to induce a feeling of flight during their religious ceremonies. Not exactly what you want to feed your family. I also omitted primrose. There is an edible primrose, *Primula vera*, that is popular in England, but it is seldom ever grown in America.

English lavender and 'Alaska' nasturtiums (*left*) line my front walk. Apple blossoms (*above*) are fragrant and tasty spring treats.

Anise hyssop

# ANISE HYSSOP
*Agastache foeniculum*

AN EXCEPTION IN THE HERB world in that it's native to the Western Hemisphere, anise hyssop is one of the most flavorful and interesting edible flowers.

**How to grow:** This highly ornamental, easily grown herbaceous perennial reaches from 3 to 6 feet and has gray-green leaves and striking, dense 1- to 3-inch flower spikes ranging from lavender to white. It is hardy to USDA Zone 4. Start anise hyssop from seeds or divisions, grow it in full sun in average soil, and keep it fairly moist. The plant dies down in the winter and often reseeds itself the next spring. It is bothered by few pests and diseases. Harvest flowers as they appear in the summer.

**How to prepare:** The young leaves and tiny petals of the sweet flowers have a flavor somewhat between anise and root beer and, if used sparingly, are very pleasant in both savory and sweet dishes. Add the petals to melted butter and serve over grilled mushrooms, use them in a beef stir-fry or a chicken marinade, or include them in a salad dressing. The natural sweetness and many complex flavors give dimension to iced drinks, custard, ice cream and sorbets, and pound cake. A few dried flower heads in the sugar bowl adds flavor to sugar for tea or sugar cookies. See the recipe for Stir-Fried Beef with Anise Hyssop on page 177.

# APPLE BLOSSOMS

*Malus* spp.

APPLE TREES PERFUME THE AIR in spring and glorify the landscape. Capture their fragrance in your desserts.

**How to grow:** Most varieties of apple trees bear light-pink to white flowers in early spring. 'Pink Pearl,' an old heirloom apple available from a few specialty fruit-tree nurseries, bears deep-pink blossoms. Buy apple trees bare root in late winter (which is when the trees are dormant with soil removed from their roots) and consult a good fruit-growing text for selecting and planting varieties appropriate for your area. Remember to keep the blossoms free of heavy-duty chemical sprays.

**How to prepare:** Apple blossoms have a slightly floral taste; the petals are lovely in salads, especially a Waldorf salad, or in a cider vinaigrette. Infuse the petals in cream for ice cream or whipped cream to go over an apple tart. You can also crystallize the petals and use them to garnish baked apples drizzled with maple syrup, applesauce, tarts, fruit soups, and French toast or crêpes filled with caramelized apples.

'Pink Pearl' apple blossoms (*top*), 'Golden Delicious' apple blossoms (*left*), 'Red Delicious' apple blossoms (*right*)

# ARABIAN JASMINE
## *Jasminum sambac*

JASMINE INVOKES IMAGES of sultry evenings in faraway places.

**How to grow:** A tender perennial vine native to tropical Asia, Arabian jasmine is hardy only in USDA Zone 10. In all other areas, it can be grown indoors with high humidity in a greenhouse. There are two Arabian jasmine cultivars of merit: 'Grand Duke of Tuscany,' which has intensely perfumed double flowers and is slow growing, and 'Maid of Orleans,' a bushy, compact plant with semidouble-white flowers. They can be obtained from mail-order nurseries specializing in tropical plants. Outside, grow Arabian jasmine in full sun or partial shade in average soil, with average watering. It is a heavy feeder, so fertilize with fish emulsion every two weeks during the growing season. When the plants are about to flower, feed them cottonseed meal or some other form of phosphorus. They grow best in temperatures of 60°F at night and 80°F during the day. Harvest the flowers just as they open.

**How to prepare:** Use the flowers to infuse simple syrups or impart their lovely perfume to tea. Use the syrup as a wonderful base for sorbets or ice creams or pour it over melons, figs, or poached pears.

'Grand Duke of Tuscany' jasmine

# ARUGULA
## *Eruca vesicaria*

ARUGULA FLOWERS ARE NUTTY and taste a bit like horseradish. Mellow and delightful, these flowers can be used in any dish that calls for arugula.

**How to grow:** Arugula is grown for its leaves; the flowers are a bonus. These cool-weather plants can be enjoyed in early spring and again in the fall. The plants are short-lived; they get quite spicy and go to flower readily in hot weather. Broadcast the seeds over rich soil in a sunny area and lightly cover them with soil, or start them in flats indoors. Keep arugula well watered and fertilize lightly. Arugula has few pest and disease problems. Harvest individual leaves when the plants are at least 4 inches tall, and the flowers as they appear. Arugula flowers attract beneficial insects, so I keep plants blooming for much of the spring. If allowed to go to seed, arugula reseeds itself readily in your garden.

**How to prepare:** Long after the leaves have become too strong tasting to use, the flowers can still be sprinkled over green or pasta salads, slivered fennel, carpaccio, frittatas, and pizzas; tucked into sandwiches filled with tomatoes or grilled mushrooms and eggplants; minced and added to a soft cheese; and used to garnish chilled tomato soup and vegetables prepared with olive oil and garlic in the Italian manner.

Arugula flowers

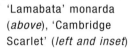

'Lamabata' monarda
(*above*), 'Cambridge
Scarlet' (*left and inset*)

# BEE BALM
(Monarda, Oswego tea)
*Monarda didyma, M. citriodora*

BEE BALM, ALSO CALLED monarda, is an exuberant plant that is native to eastern North America. In earlier times, Native Americans, and later the early settlers, used it to make tea.

**How to grow:** Bee balm produces 3-inch shaggy flowers over much of the summer. Of all the many varieties, the red cultivars seem to be the tastiest: 'Cambridge Scarlet,' 'Adam,' and 'Firecracker.' An annual monarda, 'Lamabata,' has lavender flowers and spicy petals that can be used sparingly in savory dishes, such as a green salad or cream soup, and as a garnish. Obtain monarda plants from local nurseries and mail-order firms that specialize in perennials.

Bee balm is a hardy, easy-to-grow perennial that can get to 4 feet tall. Start it with divisions planted in sun or partial shade, in moist soil. Mildew is a common problem in many climates. Harvest flowers as they appear in summer.

**How to prepare:** The flowers of the red varieties of bee balm have a fairly strong, spicy, minty taste. They are most commonly used along with the leaves to make herbal tea. Add the petals to teas and salads; sprinkle them over red snapper or other mild fish; include them in dishes with apricots, peaches, and plums; use them in the punch bowl and in fruit salads or to garnish cold drinks; or add them to apple jelly and baked goods such as pound cake.

# TUBEROUS BEGONIAS

*Begonia* X *tuberhybridia*

THESE SHOWY FLOWERS are sensational in the garden and on the table.

**How to grow:** Spectacular puffs of orange, yellow, white, pink, or red, tuberous begonia flowers range in size from 2 to 4 inches across. To ensure safe eating, either grow them without chemicals or buy chemicals that are registered for edible plants. In some climates, tuberous begonias are prone to mildew, but in many cool-summer areas these plants grow with ease. Start begonia tubers in flats or pots in the spring in rich, moist, well-draining potting soil. When the plants are 3 inches high, replant them in the garden or in containers. They need a slightly acidic soil, filtered sun, and constant moisture and feeding. Dig up the tubers in late fall, knock off the dead and dying stalks, and store the tubers in a cool, dry, frost-free place. Do not lift the tubers until the foliage turns yellow.

**How to prepare:** The flowers of most tuberous begonias have a delicious, light, lemon taste and a crisp texture. Taste them before using them to make sure they are not astringent. Use sliced petals in salads and tea sandwiches. Dip whole petals in flavored yogurt and serve as an appetizer that is sure to spark a conversation. Garnish a fish plate or a fruit or green salad with begonia petals, or use them as a spectacular garnish on an appetizer platter for a buffet.

Tuberous begonias come in a feast of colors.

# BORAGE
## *Borago officinalis*

THIS HERB, NATIVE TO EUROPE and Africa, has a slight cucumber flavor. The special blue, star-shaped flowers are lovely on salads and in cold drinks.

**How to grow:** An easily grown summer annual that sometimes acts like a biennial, borage grows to about 2 feet and has hairy, gray leaves and half-inch star-shaped deep-blue flowers. Bor-age is easily started from seeds planted in average soil and in full sun in the spring after any threat of frost is over. Harvest young leaves once the plants are established, and flowers anytime they appear. Borage often reseeds itself.

**How to prepare:** Mix the half-inch flowers in vegetable and fruit salads, especially a cucumber or jicama salad, or use them to garnish cream soups or to decorate desserts. Freeze them in ice cubes to float in iced tea. They can also be crystallized. To make the flowers edible, remove the hairy sepals using the following simple procedure. With your left hand (if you are right-handed) grasp the stem of the flower. With your right hand gently pinch the middle of the star and pull. The flower (corolla) should separate from the sepals intact.

**Caution:** Pregnant and lactating women should avoid borage flowers, as more than eight to ten flowers can cause milk to flow.

Borage flowers (*above*) are easy to harvest.

# BROCCOLI

*Brassica oleracea*

# BROCCOLI RAAB

*B. rapa (B. campestris)*

THERE ARE MANY TYPES OF broccoli: the standard heading types, sprouting broccoli, and broccoli raab—all of which produce yellow flowers—and a primitive type with very tiny buds and white flowers, called *sparachetti,* in Italy.

**How to grow:** Standard broccoli is an annual that prefers cool weather. Plant broccoli in very early spring for summer bearing, or in the summer or fall for winter bearing. Plant seeds, or place transplants in rich soil about two weeks before the last average frost date. All broccolis are heavy feeders that need a consistent supply of water and nutrients. Flea beetles, imported cabbageworm, and cutworms may be problems. Once the primary head is harvested, most broccoli varieties produce many smaller heads—the so-called sprouting broccolis produce side buds more readily than some of the modern heading varieties do.

**How to prepare:** Broccoli buds open up and produce clusters of yellow or white flowers that have a mild broccoli flavor. Incorporate them into hot pasta with broccoli florets and braised onions. Sprinkle them whole over green salads, grated carrot or cucumber salads, cold red pepper soup, gazpacho, black bean soup, and poached fish. They can also be combined with other flowers in a petal confetti.

'Sparachetti' broccoli flowers (*top*, seeds are available in Italian grocery stores and offered by Pagano's Seeds); standard broccoli (*bottom*)

131

# CALENDULA
## *Calendula officinalis*

CALENDULA, ALSO KNOWN AS pot marigold, was a popular edible flower as far back as ancient Rome, when the peasants used it as a substitute for the very expensive saffron.

**How to grow:** Calendulas are easily grown cool-season annuals that do best in fairly rich, fast-draining soil in full sun. The orange, apricot, cream, or yellow flowers can be single or double. I think the slightly sticky 2-inch green leaves have a "grassy" aroma. Tall varieties such as 'Pacific Beauty' and 'Kablouna' grow to more than 2 feet tall; dwarf varieties such as 'Bon Bon,' 'Radio,' and 'Fiesta' grow to 1 foot.

In cold-winter areas with a short spring and fall, plant seeds in flats six weeks before setting the plants outside; because calendulas can tolerate light frosts, plant calendulas in the fall in mild-winter areas. Most nurseries carry transplants in both the spring and fall. Space plants about 18 inches apart and water them in well. To keep them healthy, keep the soil evenly moist and watch for slugs and snails. Mildew is a common problem, especially in warm weather. The dwarf varieties seem to be more prone to this disease. 'Pacific Beauty' is one of the older varieties and often reseeds itself in mild climates. Other full-size varieties include the heirloom 'Radio' with its large, orange petals and the double-petaled 'Kablouna.' Two dwarf varieties, 'Fiesta' and 'Bon Bon,' have double flowers in a mix of yellow, cream, and orange. Calendulas make great cut flowers as well. For continual blooms, remove the spent flowers.

**How to prepare:** Calendula petals have a slightly tangy, bitter taste; they are often used more for their color than for their flavor. The varieties 'Pacific Beauty' and 'Radio' are easier to clean than the double varieties. To prepare calendula flowers, remove the petals from the 2- or 3-inch-wide heads and use them whole or chop them before adding them to cooked dishes such as soups, soufflés, rice dishes, muffins and biscuits, and omelets and frittatas. Vinegar infused with calendula petals and either dill or thyme makes a lovely condiment. Mince the petals to incorporate into butters and soft cheeses. To release the oils and color from the petals most effectively, include a little oil in the recipe. Whole petals can be used to garnish salads, soups, frittatas, and rice dishes. Use dried petals all winter long in soups and rice pilaf.

'Kablouna' calendulas with frost on the flowers

'Pacific Beauty' calendula flower (*top*), 'Bon Bon' calendula (*middle*), 'Pacific Beauty' plants with rosemary (*bottom*)

German chamomile

# CHAMOMILE
*Chamaemelum nobile,*
*Matricaria recutita*

THERE ARE TWO KINDS OF chamomile—the perennial type, which is low growing and moderately hardy, and an annual chamomile, which is a lovely, short-lived, garden flower.

**How to grow:** The annual chamomile, sometimes called German chamomile, grows to about 18 inches and produces a cloud of small white daisies. It has a sweeter taste and is less medicinal tasting. Many people feel that its flowers make a better tea than those from the perennial chamomile. Start both types from seeds in well-prepared soil, in full sun. Keep them fairly moist. Perennial chamomile can be grown from transplants from the nursery. It is hardy to USDA Zone 4. Both chamomiles are quite free of most pests and diseases.

**How to prepare:** Most cooks prefer the flavor of the annual chamomile. The perennial is most often used medicinally. Use the flower heads fresh or dried in herbal teas served either hot or iced. Combine the chamomile flowers with other herbs such as lemon verbena, roselle, and mint to make a more complex tea. Sprinkle the petals over salads, especially ones containing apples—the chamomile brings out their taste.

133

# CHIVES AND SOCIETY GARLIC

*Allium* spp., *and*
*Tulbaghia violacea*

HERB SOPHISTICATES AS WELL AS beginners enjoy chives. The blossoms can be used in just about any dish that calls for onions. A chive relative, society garlic grows in tufts of flat leaves and produces heads of lavender flowers that have a pronounced garlic flavor.

**How to grow:** There are two types of culinary chives: *A. schoenoprasum,* sometimes called onion chives, has a mild, onion flavor, tubular grasslike leaves to 18 inches high, and globe-shaped, lavender flowers; *A. tuberosum,* Oriental or garlic chives, is a distant relative and has an onion/garlic flavor, flat leaves to 2 feet tall, and white, star-shaped flowers. The common variety of Oriental chives blooms only once a year, producing small buds. One type of garlic chives called Chinese leek has been bred for its flower buds, which are favored in China. Its seeds are available from Evergreen Y. H. Enter-prises. Both types of chives are perennial plants hardy to USDA Zone 3.

Society garlic is a graceful plant that is used in mild-winter areas in herb gardens and as a low-maintenance, drought- and heat-tolerant ornamental. Hardy to 20°F, the plants have gray-green straplike leaves and produce 2-foot-tall flower stalks. A silver-and-white variegated form is more compact and is slow growing.

Chives and society garlic need at

Chives growing along a walk (*top left*), and a detail of chive flower (*left*); Oriental chives (*top, right*), and a detail of the society garlic flower (*bottom*)

least six hours of sun a day and average to rich, well-drained, moist soil. They are best planted in the spring; obtain divisions, purchase transplants, or grow them from seeds. Richters Herb Catalogue carries a variety of onion chives. One, 'Profusion,' is bred for its flowers, which remain edible for an extended time because they don't set seeds. (Once mature, the seed capsules produced by most varieties make the flowers feel papery in your mouth.)

Plant onion chives and the variegated society garlic in the front of, or as a border to, your herb or flower

beds and in the vegetable garden. Oriental chives and the standard society garlic, being taller, look best interplanted among other herbs and flowers or in stand-alone beds or in containers.

To keep chives growing well, apply nitrogen fertilizer in the spring or if the leaves yellow. In rainy areas supplemental watering is seldom needed. Pests, except for occasional aphids, and diseases are few and far between. Common chives bloom in early summer; most Oriental chives bloom in early fall. The Chinese leeks bloom at least twice throughout the spring and summer. Society garlic blooms from late spring to late fall.

Cut back chive plants after they flower, to renew the plant and prevent them from reseeding and becoming a nuisance. Society garlic looks best if the dead flower stalks are removed every month or so. To keep them healthy, divide your plants every three or four years.

**How to prepare:** Common chive blossoms are among the most versatile edible flowers, tasting as they do of sweet onions. Harvest the flowers just after they open, as the petals of the onion chives are pleasantly crunchy when young, but fibrous when mature. Pull apart all chive florets and sprinkle them as you would the leaves. Use the flowers in salads, sauces, or dips; make chive blossom butter to melt over vegetables; and combine the flowers with sour cream, and cream or goat cheeses. Add chive florets to herbal vinegars. Shower them over a tomato cream soup or vichyssoise, add them to a chicken stir-fry, and use them in stuffed eggs and omelets. Chinese leeks are generally blanched in the garden by cutting them to the ground and covering them to exclude the light for a few weeks—the resulting tender, yellow stalks and buds are eaten as a stir-fry vegetable. Society garlic flowers are compatible with most recipes that use garlic or onion. They are popular flowers in California wine country cuisine, where they are commonly added to salads, used as garnishes, and are spec-

tacular folded into a hot pasta dish.

# CHRYSANTHEMUMS
### *Chrysanthemum* X *morifolium, Dendranthema* X *Grandiflora*

BLOOMING CHRYSANTHEMUMS are a sign of fall, but few folks think to bring their harvest colors to the table.

**How to grow:** Chrysanthemums are perennial plants whose flowers come in nearly every color of the rainbow (except blue and a true pink or red) and range in size from 1 to 5 inches across. Buy plants in the spring from a local nursery and plant them in the garden or in containers in good soil, in full sun. To avoid spindly plants, pinch them back frequently until late summer to encourage branching. Water during dry weather. Aphids are an occasional problem. Garland chrysanthemum (shungiku greens) are grown for their greens in Asia and produce 1-inch yellow flowers with short petals.

**Caution:** Avoid nursery-grown or

Standard chrysanthemums *(top)*; 'Garland' or 'shungiku' chrysanthemums *(bottom)*

florist chrysanthemums because they are usually grown with chemicals that are not allowed on food by the USDA.

**How to prepare:** Chrysanthemum petals have a mild to strong bitter taste, depending on the variety. Use the petals in salads and tea or sprinkle them over clear soups. The varieties with large, open petals are the easiest to work with. Use the petals to garnish stir-fries and one-pot dishes.

Cilantro

# CILANTRO

(Fresh coriander)

*Coriandrum sativum*

THE PUNGENT HERB CILANTRO looks a bit like parsley but tastes very different. Some people strongly dislike the earthy flavor of the leaves and flowers, but others crave it. Known in the Americas as cilantro, or even Chinese parsley, in the Orient this herb is referred to as coriander.

Because the plants go to flower so quickly, using the flowers is a way to extend the season.

**How to grow:** This easily grown annual herb does best in cool weather. It goes to flower readily when the days start to lengthen in the spring and in warm weather. Most gardeners grow cilantro for its leaves; the flowers are just a bonus. Cilantro grown for its

leaves is best planted in the fall in all climates. In cold-winter areas the seeds sprout the next spring after the ground thaws, and in mild-winter areas the plants grow lush and tall over the winter but generally do not bloom until spring. (Cilantro tolerates light frosts.) Gardeners in short-spring areas should start with early plantings; the plants usually go to flower within 60 days.

Plant cilantro seeds $1/4$ inch deep in rich, light soil and in full sun. Thin them to 6 inches apart. Keep the plants moist to ensure lush growth. Harvest the leaves once the plants are 6 inches tall. Fertilize only if the plants get pale. Cilantro has few pests and diseases. Cilantro flowers, tiny flat sprays of white petals, are produced in profusion in the spring and summer. Not only are they edible, but they are great for attracting beneficial insects to your garden. Harvest them anytime they appear.

**How to prepare:** Cilantro leaves and flowers are almost always used raw, as the flavor fades quickly when cooked. Use whole flower heads as a garnish for green and savory vegetable salads and on cumin-sprinkled grilled chicken and fancy Southwestern spicy dishes. To incorporate the flowers into a dish, remove the small florets from the stems, which tend to be fairly tough. Chop the florets and add them sparingly to salads, quesadillas, coconut curries, stir-fries, and refried beans or fold them into cooked vegetable dishes and salsa.

# CITRUS BLOSSOMS

(Lemon and orange)

*Citrus limonia* and *C. sinensis*

THE SCENT OF CITRUS BLOSSOMS is breathtaking; being able to bring it to the table is a bonus.

**How to grow:** Lemons and oranges are evergreen shrubs or trees that bloom at different times depending on

Close-up of a lemon blossom (*top*); orange blossoms (*bottom*)

the variety. Obtain plants from local nurseries or by mail order from Logee's Greenhouses (see Resources, page 103). Plant trees in the spring in rich, well-drained soil or in containers. Keep the plants well watered and fertilize them with citrus fertilizer. Gardeners in USDA Zones 3 through 8 can grow citrus plants in a cool greenhouse in the winter and then move the plants outdoors in the summer. Spider mites and scale are occasional problems.

**How to prepare:** Many varieties of oranges have a very strong rindlike taste, but others are wonderful in syrups or jams and as a garnish. Taste a few petals before you decide how to use them. Lemon blossoms vary too. Some varieties have a strong rind taste; others, such as 'Meyer,' have a pleasant lemon taste. Use the petals to flavor whipped cream, ice cream, puddings, and lemonade—even vodka. Sprinkle these cream-colored petals on fruit salads and soups and incorporate them into a beurre blanc for fish and chicken. Use them to garnish a pork tenderloin or duck breast served with caramelized onions or over lemon-filled blintzes. If you want to candy whole citrus blossoms, a mixture of confectioners' sugar and egg whites hides the brown tinge of the petals when it dries. Apply this mix lightly and evenly and paint toward the center of the blossom, as the petals come off very easily (see "Candied Flowers," page 166).

# DAYLILIES
## *Hemerocallis* spp.

CHEERFUL DAYLILIES PRODUCE flowers that bloom for only one day—hence the name. Asians have enjoyed the blossoms for centuries.

**How to grow:** Daylilies come in all colors (except pure white and blue), including multicolor and single-color yellow, orange, and bronze; range in length from 2 to 5 inches long; and grow from 18 inches to 3 feet tall. These wonderful plants, particularly some of the older varieties, are hardy perennials that just want to grow. Buy plants from local nurseries and mail-order firms. Although you can use all varieties, the lighter-colored ones tend to be less astringent. Give all daylilies good soil in either light shade or full sun. Fertilize occasionally and keep fairly moist.

**How to prepare:** The taste of daylily petals ranges from sweet floral to slightly metallic; be sure to taste them before using them in a recipe. The buds have long been used in Chinese stir-fries and Japanese tempura. Called golden needles, the buds are traditionally chosen the day before they open for hot-and-sour soups. The buds taste like a cross between asparagus and green beans. They can also be sautéed or baked. Sliced daylily petals are used in salads and soups; once the stamens and pistils are removed, the whole flower can be stuffed with cheese or bread crumbs and sautéed, or used for a fancy wine-glass presentation of ice cream or sorbet. The sweet varieties make a tasty sorbet.

Daylily flower (*top*); daylily plants in bloom (*bottom*)

Dill flowers close up (*left*), dill growing with parsley and Johnny-jump-ups (*center*), and flowering elderberry (*right*)

# DILL

*Anethum graveolens*

DILL IS MOST FAMOUS IN pickles, but the young leaves, florets, and seeds can be used in a variety of dishes.

**How to grow:** Start these annual plants in the spring from seeds after the weather has warmed up. Plant them in full sun, in well-drained, fertile soil. These ferny plants grow to 3 feet and produce flat sprays of yellow flowers when the plants are a few months old. Keep dill moist throughout the growing season and harvest leaves as soon as the plants get 4 inches tall. Harvest flowers when they appear and use them before the florets start to turn brown.

**How to prepare:** Break up the flower heads and use them in salads and omelets; sprinkled over vegetable dishes, especially those with spinach, carrots, beets, and potatoes; in fish sauces; and with mild soft cheeses. Use the whole flower heads in jars of cucumber, snap bean, and beet pickles or to add a decorative touch in a bottle of herb-flavored vinegar.

# ELDERBERRY FLOWERS

*Sambucus canadensis, S. caerulea*

THESE EASILY GROWN SHRUBS bloom in late spring with showy, fragrant white flowers.

**Caution:** Be sure to get the cultivated edible varieties, as some of the wild, red-berried varieties are poisonous.

**How to grow:** Elderberries are easily grown deciduous shrubs that are available from local nurseries or fruit-tree specialists. It's best to plant them in out-of-the-way areas because the berries are messy, and the plants can get quite large, up to 10 feet wide. The plants grow best where the winters are cold. They need full sun, good soil, and severe annual pruning.

**How to prepare:** The cream-colored elderberry blossoms grow in large clusters. Use only the florets, as all other parts of the plants, including the stems, are poisonous. The most popular recipe for elderberry flowers is to dip the florets in a batter and cook them as fritters. The petals can also be added to jams and jellies. Dried blossoms can be used for either hot or cold tea.

# ENGLISH DAISY
*Bellis perennis*

YOU STILL FIND THE ORIGINAL English daisies growing in lawns in mild-winter areas. The ones sold in nurseries with pink, red, or white double flowers are horticultural varieties that have been selected over the years for larger and fuller flowers.

**How to grow:** English daisies are technically perennials, but they act more like biennials in mild climates and are treated as annuals in cold climates. Seldom exceeding 6 inches in height and growing from a central cluster, they thrive in full sun, moist soil, and temperate climates, where, if the spent heads are kept trimmed, they bloom again in early fall. In mild-winter areas sow the seeds directly in late summer, or set out plants in late winter. In cold-winter climates, start the seeds indoors midwinter and move plants outside after your last expected

English daisies

frost date. English daisies bloom in the spring and early summer and combine well in flower beds with tulips, pansies, and violas—all edible flowers.

**How to prepare:** The petals of the English daisy have a slightly bitter flavor and are most commonly used as a garnish sprinkled on salads, soups, and steamed vegetables.

Green fennel (*left*); Bronze fennel plants in bloom (*right*) at Well-Sweep Herb Farm in New Jersey

# FENNEL
*Foeniculum vulgare*

THIS HERB HAS BEAUTIFUL ferny foliage and lovely yellow flowers that closely resemble dill.

**How to grow:** Though a perennial, fennel is usually grown as you would dill (see page 44). There are both green and bronze types. Both grow in a similar manner. Cut back the plants in the spring to keep them looking trim. Keep the seed heads removed, as fennel reseeds itself and becomes a weed in many parts of the country. Fennel is a favorite food of the swallowtail butterfly larvae.

**How to prepare:** Use the florets to garnish dishes made with fennel; over broiled fish; in a remoulade; and chopped and added to potato, tomato, beet, and artichoke dishes.

# HONEYSUCKLE
*Lonicera japonica*

JAPANESE HONEYSUCKLE was probably one of the few flowers we grew up eating. Remember pulling the flowers off the vine and suck the sweet juice from the bottom of the flower?

**Caution:** Only the Japanese species of honeysuckle is documented as being edible.

**How to grow:** No one should be encouraged to plant Japanese honeysuckle, because this huge vine has become an invasive pest in many parts of the country. Instead, I suggest that you seek out a plant and ask the owner if you may harvest some flowers. The yellow to buff flowers bloom in late spring and sporadically throughout the summer.

**How to prepare:** The flavor of honeysuckle is but a distillation of its perfume, plus a little sweetness. Infuse the flowers by themselves or in combination with strawberries to make a sorbet, or steep them to make a hot tea. Use the whole flowers to garnish a fruit salad.

Japanese honeysuckle flowers

140

# LAVENDER

(English or French)

## *Lavandula angustifolia (officinalis)*

THE SCENT OF LAVENDER IS among the most treasured in the Western world. Few folks think of feasting on the flowers, and thus they miss the opportunity to enjoy lavender to a fuller extent.

**How to grow:** Lavender plants grow to 3 feet and are hardy to USDA Zone 5. The foliage of most lavenders is gray, and the flowers are lavender. Start lavender from cuttings or transplants and plant it in full sun. One variety, 'Lady,' starts readily from seeds and, unlike most lavenders, blooms the first year. Watering is usually needed only in arid climates and when the plant is grown in containers, and then only when the soil is fairly dry. Shear back the plants after they bloom. Like most Mediterranean herbs, lavender does poorly in heavy or poorly drained soil and succumbs to root rot readily. In hot weather, lavender occasionally becomes infested with spider mites.

Lavender flowers can be used fresh or dried. When using them fresh, cut the flower stalks and remove the tiny flowers by hand. To harvest them for drying, cut the flower stalks just as they start to bloom and hang them upside down in a warm, dark place. Remove the tiny dry flowers as you need them or take them off the stems and store them in a tightly covered container.

'Munstead' lavender

'Dwarf' English lavender

**How to prepare:** With the strong lemon-perfume taste of the petals of its 2-inch flower heads, lavender is one of the most useful culinary flowers. Leaves and flower heads can be steeped for making jellies, sorbets, caramel custard, and ice cream. Use the flowers to flavor a simple syrup that can be drizzled over poached pears or an almond tart. Lavender can be used in lemonade and vinegars and to flavor sugar, which can then be used for sweetening teas or to make shortbread or sugar cookies. (See recipe, page 90.) Traditionally, lavender buds are one of the many flavorings of herbes de Provence.

Lilac

Marigold 'Lemon Gem'

# LILACS
*Syringa vulgaris*

LILACS MARK MANY A PROPERTY line in this country, and most of us cherish the thought of their lovely perfume.

**How to grow:** Lilacs are large deciduous shrubs that bloom with lavender or white flowers in the spring in cold-winter areas. Lilacs grow poorly in warm-winter areas.

Buy plants from a nursery or order special varieties from mail-order firms. If possible, taste the variety before planting it since not all lilacs have a pleasant floral taste. Plant lilacs in neutral, fast-draining soil in a sunny location. Prune the lilac after it blooms by removing the spent flowers and shaping the shrub to keep it blooming and looking trim. To renew the plant, every few years cut some of the oldest stems almost to the ground and shorten some of the longest, lanky growth back to a strong horizontal branch. Apply a mulch of rotted manure every two years in the fall. Stem borers, leaf miners, and mildew are common problems.

**How to prepare:** Pick the flower heads soon after they open. Remove the individual florets and add them to soft cheeses or frozen yogurt or use them to garnish all sorts of sweet dishes, such as a plate of cookies, cakes, and scones.

# MARIGOLDS
*Tagetes*

SOME MARIGOLD FLOWERS can be rather smelly and unappetizing, but a few varieties have a pleasant citrus flavor.

**How to grow:** Marigolds are summer annuals that are easily grown when given fast-draining, fairly rich soil and full sun. I find 'Lemon Gem' and 'Tangerine Gem' to be the tastiest varieties. These flavorful marigolds produce clouds of $1/2$-inch flowers. There are also some light-colored varieties; 'French Vanilla' and 'Aurora Light Yellow' have a mild flavor, and the petals are useful as a garnish and in a petal confetti. Because these varieties are often not sold in local nurseries, you usually have to order seeds and start the plants yourself. Start seeds inside in the spring and transplant them after any threat of frost is over, placing them about 1 foot apart. Keep the plants fairly moist and mulch to keep them healthy. The plants will produce flowers until the fall. Young marigolds are a delicacy to slugs and snails, leaf miners sometimes tunnel through the foliage, and spider mites are sometimes a problem in hot weather.

**How to prepare:** Use marigold flowers sparingly in salads and as garnishes. Use the more flavorful 'Gem' varieties in deviled eggs, in marigold butter, sprinkled over broccoli and other assertive vegetables.

# MUSTARD

(India Mustard)

## JAPANESE RED MUSTARD, SPINACH MUSTARD

*Brassica juncea, B.* spp.

A NUMBER OF GREENS referred to as mustards produce flowers that are edible and have a slight mustard taste.

**How to grow:** Mustards are cool-season crops grown like broccoli (see page 131). Plant seeds in early spring in full sun, in rich, fertile loam. Thin to 1 foot apart. All mustards are members of the cabbage family and may occasionally be plagued by the same pests. The leaves may be harvested as needed before the plant is left to flower.

Mustard field in Germany (*above*) and mustard flower (*right*)

**How to prepare:** Mustard flowers add a little bite to a mixed salad. Use them sparingly in salads or sprinkle them on cream soups, in butters, and in dishes where broccoli flowers would be appropriate. Combine them in a salad dressed with a cider vinaigrette or use them in a remoulade. To bring out their flavor, add a little prepared mustard to the salad dressing.

143

# NASTURTIUMS

*Tropaeolum majus*

CHEERY AND PUNGENT, nasturtiums are among my favorite edible flowers. In fact, I've grown whole gardens filled with just nasturtiums.

**How to grow:** There are almost a dozen varieties of nasturtium on the market, but local nurseries usually carry only a few. Consider starting your own, as they grow best from seeds started directly in the garden. If you've never started flowers from seeds, nasturtiums are a great way to start, even for children. The select varieties include 'Alaska,' with green-and-white foliage and flowers of yellow, cream, maroon, and orange; 'Empress of India,' with deep red-orange flowers and dark-blue green leaves; 'Strawberries and Cream,' compact plants with green leaves, cream flowers, and a red throat; and 'Whirlybird,' with

green leaves and double flowers of cream, deep red, apricot, and yellow that have no spur at the back of the flower. These are all dwarf varieties that grow to about 1 foot high. There is also a large climbing mix that sprawls to 10 feet; it is sold as "climbing nasturtium" and comes in a mix of colors.

About the date of your last expected frost in the spring, plant seeds ¹/₂ inch

A section of my nasturtium garden (*top left*), 'Strawberries and Cream' nasturtiums (*top right*), 'Empress of India' nasturtiums (*bottom*)

deep in lean to average soil with good drainage. In cool-weather areas, plant them in full sun, but provide some afternoon shade in hot climates. Keep the seed bed moist. Make sure the plants don't dry out and watch for occasional aphids. Nasturtiums have a few quirks: they produce lots of flowers in lean soil and few in rich soil, and they reseed themselves heavily under favorable conditions.

**How to prepare:** The flowers, leaves, and seed pods of nasturtiums are all edible. The tangy flavor is mustardlike, with an added perfume and sweetness. Harvest the flowers just as they open. I prefer to use small leaves whole and the flowers with their petals removed, but occasionally I serve the flowers whole. They're entirely edible, just a little large. Both the leaves and the flowers are great minced and incorporated into butters and soft cheeses and used to flavor oils, dressings and vinegars, and cucumber sandwiches. The petals can be sprinkled over a green salad and used as a garnish for salads and buffet platters. Stuff whole flowers with flavored soft cheeses or guacamole. It is easier to eat the stuffed blossom on a piece of melba toast or a slice of cucumber or jicama, especially at a buffet table. To temper nasturtiums' bite, add honey or fruit juice to a dressing. The immature seed heads can be pickled and used as you would capers in salads and on pizza.

A mix of nasturtium varieties *(top)*;
'Whirlybird' nasturtium *(bottom)*

# PEAS
## *Pisum sativum*

PEA FLOWERS ARE SCULPTURAL and taste like the freshest of peas.

**Caution:** Do not confuse edible pea blossoms with sweet peas, which are poisonous.

**How to grow:** Peas are cool-season annuals that grow on either bushy plants or tall vines. All edible peas have tasty edible blossoms. Most varieties have white flowers, but a few edible pea varieties produce purple flowers, including 'Dwarf Gray Sugar.' Start peas as soon as the soil can be worked in the spring in rich, fast-draining soil in a sunny part of the garden. Plant the seeds ½ inch deep, 2 inches apart. Give the vining peas a trellis at planting time. Thin the plants to 6 inches apart and keep them moist at all times. Pea plants are prone to a number of diseases, and the seedlings are attacked by slugs, snails, and birds. Harvest some of the flowers as they appear, but don't take too many, or you will cut down on your pea production.

**How to prepare:** The flowers of some varieties have a "grassy" flavor; others have a mild, sweet, floral taste. Sprinkle them over a lobster bisque for a special garnish. Use them in a mixed or baby greens salad or as a garnish, or candy them to make some extremely pretty candied flowers great for salmon canapés or even a wedding cake.

# PINEAPPLE GUAVA
## *Feijoa sellowiana*

THE SUCCULENT PETALS OF pineapple guavas growing in my yard have won many an edible flower convert.

**How to grow:** Pineapple guava is an evergreen shrub that is native to South America and is hardy to about 20°F. In colder climates, the plants can be grown in large containers outside in the summer, to be brought in to a cool greenhouse in the winter. Plant these guavas in rich, well-drained soil, in full sun or light shade and water them moder-ately. They bloom in late spring, bearing flowers with big tufts of red stamens and five fleshy white petals. The variety that is generally available is 'Pineapple Gem.' Squirrels and some birds feast on the petals, so I cover a few branches with bird netting. Flowers left to develop produce juicy, tangy gray-green fruit about 2 inches long in midsummer.

**How to prepare:** The flowers of the pineapple guava have a sweet and tropical-guava flavor. The only part of the flower that is eaten, the petals are delicious used as a garnish to a tropical fruit salad or cold drinks, eaten with avocados, and added to tropical jellies and fruit salsas.

'Dwarf Gray Sugar' pea blossoms (*top*), 'Tall Telephone' blossoms (*middle*), a pineapple guava flower (*bottom*)

# PINKS

*Dianthus* spp.

PINKS WERE POPULAR IN OUR grandmothers' day and often lined a front walk or flower bed.

**How to grow:** Though called pinks, dianthus has pink, rose, white, or red flowers. Pinks are easily grown perennials that are at home in a rock garden or flower border. They are hardy, and some varieties bloom most of the summer. They grow best in full sun, in rich, well-drained soil. Start them from seeds or divisions, or buy plants from the nursery. The best-tasting ones are the small, fragrant clove pinks, *D. caryophyllus,* or cottage pinks, *D. plumarius.*

**How to prepare:** Pinks have a pleasant spicy, floral, clovelike taste. The 1- to 2-inch blossoms can be steeped in wine; made into syrup, sorbets, or custard; chopped and mixed into butter; and used to garnish cakes, salads, soups, and the punch bowl. Taste your flowers first: sometimes the white base of the petals is bitter. If so, remove it.

# RADISHES

*Raphanus sativus*

RADISH FLOWERS COME in pink, lavender, and white. They are produced when the plants are allowed to bolt but before they go to seed, a frequent occurrence since the plants are so short-lived.

**How to grow:** Obviously, the point of growing radishes is to produce the roots; the flowers are just a bonus. Sow seeds directly in the garden after the last frost, or sow them in early fall. Radishes prefer cool weather. Plant seeds 1/2 inch deep, and thin to 2 inches apart. The soil should be light and well drained. Keep the young radishes constantly moist. Most varieties are ready in a month and bloom a few weeks later. In some areas of the country radishes are bothered by root maggots. Flea beetles can also be a considerable problem.

**How to prepare:** Harvest the small flower spikes and put them in water until you are ready to serve them. Remove the individual flowers from the stems and sprinkle them over a salad or over cooked vegetables. Radish flowers can be used in the same way as broccoli and mustard flowers (see pages 37 and 49). In addition, use them in a salad of julienned daikon to enhance the flavor and give color.

Dianthus 'Horatio' (*top*), Cottage pinks (*middle*); radish flowers (*bottom*) are not only tasty; they attract beneficial insects such as this syphid fly

147

Redbud (*left*) and Rosemary 'Tuscan Blue' (*right*)

# REDBUD

(Judas Tree)

*Cercis canadensis,*
*Cercis siliquastrum*

REDBUDS ARE LOVELY, SMALL trees with spectacular magenta flowers in the spring and rounded, gray-green leaves throughout the summer.

**How to grow:** Redbuds bloom in early spring. Plant them in full sun or partial shade, in sandy loam. They grow well under larger trees in a woodland garden and in cold climates, as they need some winter chill to flower profusely. Redbuds are available from local nurseries. Varieties to look for include 'Flame,' which has double pink flowers; 'Rubye Atkinson,' with its pure pink flowers; and 'Silver Cloud,' which has marbled foliage. Harvest the flower spikes and break off the small flowers before serving.

**How to prepare:** Redbud flowers can be picked either as buds or when in full flower. They have long been popular in Italy. Buds can be pickled in vinegar, like capers. Make the flower clusters into fritters and fry them in batter. They also add a pleasant crunch to salads or can be used as a garnish for cooked vegetables. The flavor is a cross between green beans and a tart apple.

# ROSEMARY

*Rosmarinus officinalis*

ROSEMARY IS A PUNGENT, resinous herb native to the Mediterranean.

**How to grow:** A tender perennial, rosemary needs full sun and fast-draining soil. In USDA Zones 8 and colder, it is usually grown as an annual or planted in containers and brought inside for the winter. Most varieties produce a profusion of light-blue flowers in the spring, but other colors include deep blue, lavender, pink, and white.

The standard culinary rosemary has light-blue flowers, as does 'Arp,' which is reputed to be the hardiest variety, to 10°F; 'Irene' and 'Tuscan Blue' have dark-blue flowers; and 'Majorca Pink' has pink ones. You can purchase the unusual varieties from specialty herb nurseries.

Gardeners everywhere have trouble with root rot if the drainage is poor, and spider mites are occasionally a problem in hot weather or when rosemary is grown inside. Gardeners in the South may have problems with nematodes. Harvest the flowering stems or individual flowers.

**How to prepare:** The small and slightly resinous flowers make a lovely confetti to sprinkle over salads and vegetable dishes. Rosemary flowers are compatible with many dishes containing pork, duck, and lamb and can be sprinkled over salmon, scallops, and swordfish; included in a pilaf; added to a butter sauce to dress grilled eggplants and mushrooms; or used on top of roasted potatoes. The flowers can also be added to herb vinegars. Whole flowering stems can be used to garnish a buffet platter.

# ROSES

*Rosa* spp.

ROSE FLOWERS HAVE BEEN USED in cooking since ancient times in both Europe and Asia.

**How to grow:** Rose flowers come in a range of colors, from red through yellow. All are edible, but the heirlooms such as *Rosa gallica,* the gallicas; *R. moschata*, the musk roses; *R. centifolia,* the centifolia or cabbage roses; and *R. damascena,* the damask roses, are usually the most hardy, disease resistant, and fragrant; thus they are usually the most flavorful. Most of these heirloom roses grow to be very large plants and, with few exceptions, bloom only in the spring.

Other roses you might choose from include 'Cécile Brünner,' a small, pink sweetheart rose; 'Zéphirine Drouhin,' a very fragrant, bright pink rose; 'Austrian Copper,' a deep orange single rose; 'Eglantine,' a small, deep pink rose that smells like apples; 'Belinda,' a small, deep-pink rose particularly good for candying whole; *Rugosa alba,* a hardy, lovely, fragrant, white, single flower that's one of the tastiest and best for sorbet. All are quite disease resistant and need little spraying in most climates. Again, most bloom only once in the spring, though a few give a sparse bloom in late summer. Other roses that have little fragrance but are lovely for garnishing include 'The

Roses, clockwise from top: 'Perfect Moment,' an old moss rose, 'Iceberg,' Luther Burbank's rose, the deep-orange 'Austrian Copper,' and 'Graham Thomas'

'The Fairy' (*left*) and 'Pink Flower Carpet' and 'Red Meidiland' roses (right)

Fairy,' 'Carefree Delight,' and 'Jeanne Lajoie.' Varieties I've enjoyed that take more care but are tasty and beautiful and bloom all summer are 'Graham Thomas' and 'Perfect Moment.'

Cathy Barash, edible flower maven, who grows roses extensively in USDA Zone 5, likes to recommend 'Tiffany,' 'Mr. Lincoln,' 'Double Delight,' 'Mirandy,' and 'Pink Flower Carpet' (which is not fragrant but has a pleasant taste) as fairly hardy if given winter protection, good for the kitchen, and resistant to diseases in the New York area. They all bloom throughout the summer.

Rosebushes are best planted bare root in early spring. Appendices A and B (pages 184-195) give basic information on planting and maintaining

the easy-care old roses and some of the modern landscape roses. If you choose some of the hybrid tea and florabunda roses, chances are they will need much extra care—fertilizing and substantial disease and pest controls—so you will need to consult some books on roses (see the Bibliography, page 199) to keep them growing well.

**Caution:** Never eat florist-grown roses, as they usually contain toxic chemicals.

**How to prepare:** Most rose varieties have a strong floral taste. Some of the dark-red varieties can be too strong and metallic tasting. With most roses, you need to remove the white part at the base of the petal, as it is bitter.

Individual petals of large varieties and the whole small-flowered roses can be candied and used as a garnish on desserts. Use fragrant rose petals to make jellies, rose water, and vinegars. They can be infused to make flavored honey, butters, and simple and fruit syrups; sprinkled over salads; placed under a sorbet to create a graceful presentation; and used in many ways as a garnish. To make rose sugar, mince 2 cups of fragrant petals and pound them together with a mortar and pestle with 1 cup of granulated sugar. Let the mixture sit for a week, strain out the petals, and store the sugar in an airtight container.

# RUNNER BEANS

*Phaseolus coccineus*

RUNNER BEANS ARE DRAMATIC vines that are covered most of the summer with spikes of small, red flowers.

**How to grow:** Runner beans are grown for their dramatic, long string beans, which are eaten fresh or allowed to dry and then stored for later use. The flowers are just a bonus. These beans grow best in cool-summer areas, and most varieties have large vines with flowers of red orange, white, or, in the case of 'Painted Lady,' salmon and white. A dwarf variety, 'Scarlet Bees,' grows to 2 feet and has red flowers. Grow runner beans as you would most snap beans— in good soil, in full sun. Plant the seeds 1 inch deep, 3 inches apart. Thin them to 6 inches apart. Keep the plants fairly moist and protect the seedlings from slugs, snails, and bean beetles. The plants flower within a few months and produce beans if the weather stays near 80°F. When temperatures get high, the plants usually produce some flowers but no beans.

Scarlet runner beans (*top left*), 'Scarlet Bees' runner beans (*top right*), safflower (*above*)

**How to prepare:** Runner bean flowers have a sweet, bean/pea taste and a slightly crunchy texture. Use them to top soups, especially bean soups; in cream-cheese appetizer sandwiches; in green and bean salads; and as a garnish for steamed snap beans and white bean puree.

# SAFFLOWER

*Carthamus tinctorius*

SAFFLOWERS ARE TALL, STIFF plants with 1-inch thistle-like flowers.

**How to grow:** Safflower is a tender annual that grows to 3 feet tall. It prefers light, dry, well-drained soil. Plant seeds every 6 inches, about $1/2$ inch deep, after any danger of frost is past. Thin the seedlings to 2 feet apart. Safflower needs full sun. Safflower blooms in midsummer with thistle-shaped flowerheads that turn from deep yellow to deep red as they mature. They have few pest and disease problems.

**How to prepare:** Safflower petals taste slightly bitter. Remove the petals from the tops of the flowers and use them fresh or dried. In either form the petals give cooked foods a lovely yellow color. Substitute safflower for calendula petals in recipes such as poor man's rice, or sprinkle them over a carrot salad or sliced jicama.

Saffron flowers among lambs' ears leaves

# SAFFRON

*Crocus sativus*

PROBABLY ONE OF THE world's most expensive flavorings, the spice consists of the dried, pulverized stigmas of a fall-blooming crocus.

**How to grow:** Plant the corms of these crocuses in late summer. They are available from a few specialty seed companies and nurseries. Hardy to USDA Zone 6, these plants prefer rich, well-drained soil with some afternoon shade. Plant these pretty, mauve to purple crocuses in large quantities if you wish to harvest them for the saffron, since a suitable harvest requires many plants. Divide and replant every two years.

**Caution:** Do not confuse saffron crocus with the autumn crocus, *Colchicum*, which is poisonous.

**How to prepare:** Remove the orange stigmas with tweezers, dry them for a few days, and store them in a covered jar in a warm, dry place. Grind and use them in rice dishes, including pilaf and paella; with seafoods; and in East Indian dishes. Saffron also adds a gorgeous golden color to bundt cakes and the famous French fish soup bouillabaisse.

# SAGE

*Salvia officinalis, S. elegans*

SAGE FLOWERS ARE spectacular spikes of purple or red flowers; they taste like the leaves, only a little sweeter. Not all culinary sages bloom, so look for specific varieties that have flowers.

**How to grow:** Most culinary sages are perennials that are grown from cuttings. Common sage is hardy to USDA Zone 4 if given protection in the coldest regions. Pineapple sages are hardy only to USDA Zone 7. Most sages do poorly in hot, humid climates and are treated as annuals in the Deep South. Plant sage in average soil with extremely good drainage and in full sun. In hot weather, and on house-grown sages, spider mites are occasionally a problem. For the best flower selection, plant the standard culinary sage, with its gray leaves and spikes of purple or white flowers, in the spring, and pineapple sage, in either its full size or dwarf version with its green leaves and red flower spikes, in the fall. To keep these plants looking neat, trim them back once heavily in the spring and, if leggy, again in the summer. Harvest whole flowering spikes or individual florets.

Common purple sage *(top)* and the less-common white variation *(bottom)*

**How to prepare:** The flower spikes of common sage are great dipped in a tempura batter and deep-fried. Use individual florets to garnish saltim-bocca, carpaccio, roast venison, white bean or tomato cream soup, and frit-tatas. Sprinkle them over a green tossed salad, steamed mussels, or a fennel and orange salad. Add them to a wild mushroom risotto, mince the blossoms and incorporate them into a cheddar or cream cheese spread, or use them in sweet butter to melt over pork or grilled mushrooms. The red spikes of pineapple sage flowers have a distinctive pineapple taste; the individual florets can be used in teas and cold drinks and in tropical fruit salads, jams, jellies, and salsas.

A collection of scented geraniums at the Berkeley Botanical Garden (*above*) and lemon-scented geranium (*right*)

# SCENTED GERANIUMS
## *Pelargonium* spp.

SCENTED GERANIUMS HAVE small, edible flowers that are generally pink to rose.

**How to grow:** The many names of scented geraniums belie their taste. Lemon, mint, chocolate, nutmeg, and rose geraniums produce edible flowers. Only the rose- and lemon-scented ones are worth using in the kitchen, however.

Set out plants from the nursery after the weather warms up, or start them from cuttings earlier in the spring. In climates where winter temperatures stay above 30°F, they can be grown outside year-round. Gardeners in cold climates grow them in containers and bring them inside for the winter. The plants can grow to 3 feet across in mild climates and benefit from annual pruning to keep them neat looking. Plant scented geraniums in full sun or light shade, in well-drained soil. Fertilize and water only occasionally. Harvest individual small flower clusters off the plant and separate them before serving them.

**How to prepare:** Use the small flowers of rose and lemon geraniums to flavor ice creams and custards or to garnish a fruit salad. Add them to crème fraîche served over strawberries or peaches. Flavor apple jelly with them, and use the jelly between layers

of pound cake or as a glaze on a fruit tart. Florets can also be put into a sugar canister to flavor sugar for use in pound cake, sugar cookies, and tea. My greatest success at candying edible flowers has been with scented geraniums; they keep their color and are very flavorful.

A basket of squash blossoms (*top*); 'Gold Rush' zucchini blossoms (*bottom*); notice the baby squash at the back of the female flowers

154

# SQUASH BLOSSOMS
## *Cucurbita* spp.

ALL SQUASH AND PUMPKINS produce large, yellow blossoms that are edible. These flowers have a long history as a delicacy reaching back to the early Native American tribes.

**How to grow:** All squash are warm-weather crops that grow well in a vegetable garden. Zucchini squash produces the most, and largest, blossoms. Try in particular the varieties 'Clarimore' and 'Gold Rush.' Plant squash seeds 1 inch deep in the spring after any threat of frost has passed. Have the soil filled with well-rotted manure. All squash need full sun. The bush types spread to 3 feet; the large winter squash and pumpkins spread to 12 feet. Keep the soil moist and fertilize midseason with fish meal or emulsion. Where cucumber beetles and squash vine borers are a problem, cover the plants with floating row covers until the blossoms appear.

Try to gather the blossoms in the early morning before they close, and put their bases or stems in water in the refrigerator until you need them. The female flowers have an immature little squash at the base where they meet the stem; the male flowers end at the stem. Most gardeners gather only male blossoms, making sure to leave a few to pollinate the females. If you need to harvest all the male flowers, you can hand-pollinate the remaining females. With a cotton swab or small paintbrush, gently rub the anthers on a male flower to obtain pollen. One by one, transfer the pollen to the centers of the female flowers. To slow down summer squash production, to thin a winter squash harvest, or when you are cooking the blossoms as baby squash, harvest females too.

**How to prepare:** Squash blossoms have a slightly sweet nectar taste. Wash and gently dry the flowers. (Watch out for bees if you are using closed blossoms; the bees sometimes get trapped inside and, contrary to reason, are not happy when you free them!) If you're using the blossoms for fritters or stuffing, keep the stems on. Stuff them with cheeses, bread crumbs, couscous, or meat mixtures and bake or deep-fry them. Don't worry about the sharp prickles—they will wilt during cooking. Otherwise, remove stems, stamens, and stigmas. Some cooks string the blossoms like celery, removing the veins that run down the outside of the flower. Thinly slice the blossoms and use them in cream soups, soufflés, frittatas, omelets, scrambled eggs, burritos; over pasta; and sprinkled on salads accompanied by a pumpkin seed oil vinaigrette.

'Pink Panda' strawberry flowers (*left*);
'Sequoia' strawberry flowers (*right*)

# STRAWBERRIES

*Fragaria* X *ananassa*

WE GROW STRAWBERRIES for their luscious fruits, but the white single flowers are also edible.

**How to grow:** Grow strawberries in a vegetable garden in full sun in rich organic soil that is fairly moist. They are hardy to USDA Zone 4. Runners are available from the nursery in the spring. Choose locally adapted, day-neutral or ever-bearing varieties, as they produce for most of the summer. 'Pink Panda' produces lots of pink flowers and few fruits. Plant 1 foot apart. Mulch strawberry plants well and fertilize mid-season with fish emulsion. Harvest occasional flowers and fruits as they appear.

Slugs attack both flowers and fruits. During hot weather, strawberries are prone to spider mites, and the plants will rot if the drainage is poor.

**How to prepare:** Sprinkle strawberry petals over salads and candy them whole to use as a garnish for all sorts of desserts.

# THYME

*Thymus* spp.

THYME IS A FRAGRANT HERB from the Mediterranean that produces clouds of small, edible flowers.

**How to grow:** Thyme is hardy to USDA Zone 5, though it needs a protective mulch in the coldest zones. These spreading perennials vary from 4 to 12 inches high and are gray green, dark green, or golden. French thyme, *T. vulgaris,* is the most commonly used culinary thyme and has lavender flowers. Other choice varieties are lemon thyme, *T. citriodorus,* which has a rich lemon taste and pink flowers; and caraway thyme, *T. herba-barona,* with a caraway taste and pink flowers. All thymes need full sun and fast-draining soil. In the spring cut back the foliage by about a third so the plant stays lush. Most gardeners start plants with transplants. Thymes are quite pest and disease resistant.

**How to prepare:** The tiny pink or lavender flowers are borne on sprigs

'Lime,' 'French,' 'Wooly' thyme and dianthus

that are great for garnishing plates and platters. The small flowers can be removed from the stems and sprinkled over soups, salads, sauces, braised rabbit, grilled or poached fish, grilled duck breast, asparagus, and caramelized sweet onions, or they can be incorporated into soft cheeses and butters.

# TULIPS
## *Tulipa* spp.

TULIPS ARE BELOVED HARBINGERS of spring. The flowers can be red, yellow, orange, magenta, pink, lavender, or white, and fluted or smooth.

**How to grow:** Purchase bulbs at your local nursery. Tulips are hardy plants grown from bulbs set out in fall. Before planting, prepare the bed well and add bonemeal. In large drifts or even in containers, plant the bulbs two and a half times as deep as they are wide. Make the beds in a sunny area in well-draining soil. If rodents are a problem, plant the bulbs in wire baskets and cover the emerging spring shoots with netting.

**Caution:** A few people are allergic to tulips, so all new diners should proceed with caution. Look for numb hands or an upset stomach.

**How to prepare:** Tulip petals have a sweet, pealike flavor and a tender, crisp texture. Use them in salads or tea sandwiches. Try arranging the petals on a platter around your favorite savory dip. Or better yet, stuff whole flowers with shrimp or chicken salad for a showstopper. Carefully remove the pollen and stigmas from the base of the flowers before stuffing them.

'Balalaika' red, 'Delyne Goldtech' orange, and yellow 'Jewel of Spring' tulips (*top*);
'Big Chief' tulips (*bottom*)

# VIOLAS, PANSIES, AND JOHNNY-JUMP-UPS

*Viola cornuta, V. wittrockiana,* and *V. tricolor*

THE FRIENDLY FACES OF VIOLAS and pansies appear in almost all climate zones during the cool season.

**How to grow:** These viola-type flowers come in various colors and are about $\frac{1}{2}$ inch to 3 inches across, depending on the variety. They are all annual flowers that grow best in cool weather. Plant seeds or bedding plants in moist, rich soil, in partial shade. They can take light frost. Fertilize every six weeks with fish emulsion. To keep the flowers coming, remove the old flower heads every few weeks. The 'Universal' pansy and 'Crystal Bowl' violas are the varieties most readily available. The most notable pests are slugs, snails, earwigs, and sowbugs, which eat the emerging buds, and various rots that attack in humid weather. Johnny-jump-ups will generally reseed themselves in your garden.

**How to prepare:** The petals have a very slight lettuce-like taste. They are beautiful for decorating desserts, as garnishes, and in salads. They can be made into a flavorful, simple syrup or they can be candied. When infused in a vinegar, the purple flowers turn the mixture lavender.

A mix of 'Universal' pansies (*above*); Johnny-jump-ups (*bottom*)

# VIOLETS
## *Viola odorata*

CANDIED VIOLETS HAVE BEEN a treat for centuries and are still available in gourmet shops today.

**How to grow:** These hardy perennials grow well in a shady, moist corner of the garden in rich soil. The single, so-called wild species of violets grows so readily that it can become a nuisance. You can also obtain many selected cultivars that come in purple, pink, or white. As a rule, these varieties are much less vigorous, and some have no fragrance. Buy the common violets and an occasional named variety at your local nursery, and, if possible, buy them in bloom to ensure they are fragrant. You can probably get divisions of the common violet from a gardening friend. Spider mites can sometimes be a problem in dry climates.

**How to prepare:** Violets have a strong, sweet, very floral taste. They're great for candying or using plain in desserts, salads, garnishes, and tea sandwiches. Freeze them in ice cubes and float them in a punch bowl. Use violets to scent a sugar bowl, flavor a custard, or color and flavor a vinegar.

Orange 'Crystal Bowl' violas with the edible flowers of mâche (*top*); harvest of pansies and violas (*bottom*); common violets (*facing page*)

158

# favorite
## flower
## recipes

I remember the first time an artichoke was placed in front of me. I had never seen one, and a knife and fork looked woefully inadequate. "How do you eat it?" I asked my hostess. Over the years I have had a similar feeling when restaurants put flowers on my plate. Flower eating is not part of our culinary heritage, but in many other cultures, both ancient and modern, people grow up eating flowers without thinking it odd at all. The Japanese and Chinese put chrysanthemum blossoms in tea, Italians regularly use squash blossoms, and other Europeans have used roses and violets for centuries. In fact, much of the information in the "Encyclopedia of Edible Flowers" (page 123) was drawn from historical documents and ethnic cookbooks.

I gathered the following recipes partly from those sources, partly from some of this country's best cooking professionals, and partly from my own experience. Unfortunately, I couldn't begin to incorporate all the ways of preparing edible flowers, but you'll get a good foundation. You'll also discover that you can get very involved without using complicated cooking techniques and that the range of possibilities is

exhilarating. Even very simple uses of flowers can be quite spectacular—chopping up rose petals and incorporating them into sweet butter, for example, or decorating baked pears with white lilac florets. Consider making such dishes as baklava flavored with rose petal honey, herb pizza sprinkled with nasturtium and herb flowers, a wedding cake strewn with fresh violets or orange blossoms, or sorbet made with cottage pinks or apple blossoms.

Flowers in the kitchen are indisputably primarily decorative—their colors and shapes are truly spectacular additions. American cooks are beginning to think more and more about how food is presented and to subscribe to the belief that beautiful meals are more satisfying and life-enhancing than plain fare. Consider how much more festive and colorful are salads made with borage and nasturtium blossoms than those sporting the usual

Edible flowers *(left)* ready to garnish a buffet table full of salads include calendulas, chives, mustard flowers, and scented geraniums.

radish or red cabbage slices. Parsley has been done to death, so how about using mustard or scarlet runner bean blossoms instead? Or for an alternative to the usual frosting flowers on your next birthday cake, how about using violets or honeysuckle blossoms or large damask rose petals?

But eye appeal is not the only virtue of edible flowers. Many actually give us new flavors to cook with. Consider the rich aroma of roses, lavender, orange blossoms, or anise hyssop.

The "Encyclopedia of Edible Flowers" resolves the most important issue of which flowers are edible, but some fundamental questions remain: How are the flowers prepared for cooking? What parts are edible? Which flowers go with which dishes?

First, taste some of the flowers to see if you like them. This step may seem obvious, but I've been served some pretty unpalatable flowers over the years—I'm sure the cooks hadn't tasted them beforehand. Pick the flowers in the cool of the day, preferably in the morning. Put those with long stems in water; pick short-stemmed ones, such as borage and orange blossoms, no more than three or four hours ahead of time, put them between layers of damp paper towels or in a plastic bag, and refrigerate. Flowers, of course, are perishable and wilt in a warm place. And they'll bruise almost instantly if they're handled roughly.

Most cooks gently wash flowers before using them. Especially for candying, flowers must be thoroughly dry, so allow an hour or so for the flowers to dry. While washing your flowers, look for "critters," such as baby slugs, earwigs, and thrips, that might be hiding down in the petals. There are more places to hide in flowers than in vegetables, and many people get really upset when they see something crawl out of their salad.

With some flowers—such as roses, calendulas, tulips, chrysanthemums, and lavender—only the petals are edible. With others—Johnny-jump-ups, violets, and pea and runner bean blossoms—the whole flower can be eaten. Separate the petals just before you use them, as they wilt within minutes. Some flower petals, such as those of roses, dianthus, and marigolds, have a white part that can be quite bitter; remove it. Also remove the stamens, styles, and sepals of large flowers such as tulips, open lilies, and squash blos-

soms because they are usually too tough.

It is important for the flowers to fit the dish. While not an absolute rule, sweet flowers are best in or as garnishes to desserts and fruit dishes, and savory types are wonderful with soups, salads, and entrées. For example, use chive blossoms in sandwiches and on onion dishes, nasturtiums in salads, and mustard blossoms on ham-filled crepes. The sweet, floral taste of roses, violets, and apple blossoms goes well with cakes, puddings, and pies. Bee balm petals are rather floral and sweet but make a good garnish to a lemon-flavored fish sauce. Use discretion with

garnishes; the flavor of the flower shouldn't overpower the dish. Lavender, for instance, is very strong, and a whole flower on a light cream soup would probably obliterate the taste of the soup. A few tiny lavender petals or mild calendula petals would be a subtle and elegant solution.

Use squash blossoms in crepes, light soups, and omelets. Steep lavender and apple blossoms as well as honeysuckle, anise hyssop, and violets in milk and then use the milk to make a custard for pies, puddings, ice cream, or for filling for cream puffs. Imagine floating-island pudding with a violet-flavored custard and meringues deco-

rated with candied violets. Even more lusciously decadent is a Grand Marnier chocolate cake decorated with orange blossoms. Use flower butters on pasta, bread, tea sandwiches, and biscuits. Use candied flowers throughout the year on mousses, soufflés, chiffon and cream pies, chocolate truffles, petits fours, hors d'oeuvres, ice creams, iced teas, and all kinds of cakes.

Classic tea sandwiches (*left*) are filled with watercress and cream cheese. Blue violas and white watercress blossoms are tucked into the sandwiches and used to garnish the plate. Rose-scented geranium jelly can be used between layers of pound cake or piped into delicate rolled cookies to make little treats to serve at a shower or fancy party (*above*).

# Flower Butters

Both savory and sweet butters can be made with flowers. Probably the most versatile savory butters are made from chive blossoms or nasturtium flowers. Serve these savory butters with a crisp French bread or melt them over vegetables, fish, or poultry. Or also add savory herbs, lemon juice, or other flavorings such as ground chipotle peppers or grated fresh ginger. Sweet flower butters can be made with roses, violets, lavender, and pineapple sage and are a treat on egg breads, sugar cookies, or as a mystery filling between layers of pound or sponge cake.

### Nasturtium Butter

4 ounces unsalted butter (1 stick),
 room temperature
12 to 18 nasturtium flowers

2 to 4 fresh nasturtium leaves, or a
 few sprigs of fresh parsley
3 or 4 chive leaves (optional)

### Chive Blossom Butter

4 ounces unsalted butter (1 stick),
 room temperature
10 to 12 large, barely open common chive flowers, florets (petal
 clusters) separated
2 small sprigs of fresh parsley, or 8
 or 10 large chive leaves

### Rose Butter

4 ounces unsalted butter (1 stick),
 room temperature
1 teaspoon superfine sugar, or finely
 granulated sugar (sometimes
 called bartenders' sugar)
$^1/_4$ teaspoon almond extract
Generous handful of rose petals from
 the fragrant old-fashionned types,
 such as 'Belle of Portugal,' any of
 the rugosa roses and damasks, and
 the 'Eglantine' rose (enough to yield
 2 tablespoons of chopped petals)

Making any flower butter involves the same process. First, remove the petals from the flowers and wash them well in cold water—check for critters. Gently pat them dry in a towel or dry them in a salad spinner. Using a very sharp knife, mince the flowers and any leaves. (Mincing is easier if you roll the blossoms into a small ball before cutting them.) Cut a stick of room-temperature butter into six or eight pieces and then mash them with a fork. When the butter is fairly soft, slowly incorporate any flavorings and the flowers and leaves. With a rubber spatula put the mixture into a small butter crock or decorative bowl. Refrigerate until serving time. Flower butters can be frozen in sealed containers for up to two months.

All three recipes make a little more than $^1/_2$ cup.

# Sweet Things

## Lavender Sugar

Making fragrant lavender sugar takes about a month. Use it to flavor cookies, lemonade, and hot or cold teas.

- ¹/₂ cup dried lavender leaves and flowers
- 2 cups superfine sugar, or finely ground granulated sugar (sometimes called bartenders' sugar)

In a jar with a tight lid, mix the dried lavender and the superfine sugar. Shake it up occasionally to equally distribute the sugar. After about three weeks to a month the oils of the lavender will have flavored the sugar sufficiently. Sift the mixture through a large strainer to remove the lavender. Store the sugar in its jar for up to a year.

Makes 2 cups.

## Rose Petal Honey

Robin Sanders and Bruce Naftaly of Le Gourmand restaurant in Seattle use this honey to make baklava, transforming an already delicious dessert into something divine. They also suggest using this honey in other desserts, meat glazes, and tea. When using rose honey in your favorite baklava recipe (*Joy of Cooking* has one; eliminate the orange water, though), also sprinkle a few chopped honeyed rose petals on the nut mixture and use fresh or candied roses as garnish.

- 1 cup unsprayed rose petals, preferably the fragrant old-fashioned types, such as 'Belle of Portugal,' any of the rugosa roses, damasks, and the eglantine rose
- 1 cup honey

Rinse the rose petals briefly in cold water and dry them in a salad spinner. In a nonaluminum pan, slowly heat the honey until runny. With a wooden spoon stir in the rose petals, cover, and steep over extremely low heat for 45 minutes, stirring occasionally. Remove from heat and let cool for 15 minutes. Strain the honey through a fine sieve, and reserve petals for another use.

Makes about 1 cup.

## Quick Rose-Scented Geranium Apple Jelly

This is one of Carole Saville's creations. Her favorite way to use the jelly is to make pound cake "sandwiches." If you want a more strongly flavored jelly, add another scented geranium leaf to the recipe.

- ¹/₄ cup fresh raspberries
- 3 large rose-scented geranium leaves
- 1 (10-ounce) jar apple jelly
- Petals from 18 rose-scented geranium flowers

Place the raspberries in a strainer placed over a small bowl. With the back of a spoon mash the berries against the side of the strainer to extract the juice. Set the juice aside.

Wash and thoroughly dry the geranium leaves. Finely chop the leaves and tie them in a square of cheesecloth.

Pour the apple jelly into a saucepan and quickly bring it to a boil. Stir in the reserved raspberry juice, then add the bag of geranium leaves. Stir the mixture for 1 minute, then cover tightly, and remove from heat. Let the jelly cool for about 20 minutes. Uncover the pan and, with the back of a spoon, press the bag of geranium leaves against the side of the pan to extract all the juice. Discard the bag of geranium leaves. Stir in the geranium petals. Pour the still-warm jelly into a hot, sterilized jar. Put on the lid and allow the jelly to cool (it should take approximately an hour). Refrigerate and use within two weeks.

Makes 10 ounces.

## Tip:

"I add an extract of roses to a standard angel food cake and cover with a pale-pink icing. I then decorate the cake with fresh roses and violets and put rose geranium leaves around the base. I serve it with ice cream and a little bit of crème de cassis (a black-currant liqueur) so that everything is pale pink."

—Holly Shimizu, managing director of the Lewis Ginter Botanical Garden in Richmond, Virginia

# Candied Flowers

Baby roses, Johnny-jump-ups, violets, violas, scented geraniums, orange blossoms, edible pea blossoms (not sweet peas, which are poisonous), and borage are all particularly well suited to candying.

Use candied flowers to decorate cakes, cookies, ice cream, and hors d'oeuvres. Wedding cakes are stunning covered with candied roses, and salmon canapés are dramatic decorated with candied pea blossoms. For an Art Deco presentation, cover a cake with marzipan icing, wrap it with blue French ribbon, and create a cluster of matte-finish, blue-candied pansies.

In the cool of the morning on a dry day, select and cut flowers that are perfectly shaped and newly opened. Keep enough of their stems so you can put them in water and later hold them comfortably. Wash the flowers a few hours before working with them so they will be dry.

To candy flowers, you need a small paintbrush, a bowl, cake rack, fork, finely ground granulated sugar (sometimes called bartenders' sugar or superfine sugar), and an egg white.

In a small bowl, beat an egg white only slightly. Holding a flower by its stem, gently paint the petals with a light coating of egg white, thoroughly covering the front and back because any part of the petal not covered will wither and discolor. Sprinkle the flowers with sugar, making sure to cover both sides of the petals thoroughly. An

To candy violets *(top)* or other edible flowers, first give them a light coating of egg white with a paint-brush, being careful to completely cover the petals. With your fingers, lightly sprinkle extra-fine granulated sugar over the petals. Dry them on a rack in a very warm, dry place for a few days or in a dehydrator until firm. Once the flowers are dry *(bottom)*, put them in a flat, dry container. Use the flowers to decorate cakes and cookies. Any

alternative method is to use a paste mixture of confectioners' sugar and a little egg white. This mixture gives a matte finish to citrus blossoms and large flowers like dark-colored pansies. Paint this mixture on both sides of the petals.

When your flower is completely sugared, lay it on a cake rack and spread the petals in a natural position. After an hour or two move the flowers around so the petals won't stick to the rack. Put the flowers in a warm, dry place (I use my gas oven, with just the heat from its pilot light) or in a food dehydrator set on low. After a few days they should be fully dry; store them in a sealed tin. Some of the flowers will become deformed; discard them or break them up to use as a confetti. You can use your candied flowers immediately, but if you store them in a dry place, most varieties will keep for up to a year.

broken pieces of candied flowers can be used to sprinkle on confections as you would confetti, shown on the cake in the same photo, to the right. When you candy flowers, if you use confectioners' instead of granulated sugar you can achieve a matte finish on the flowers, giving them a delicate, old-fashioned look. The cake here (*far right*) has been garnished with yellow pansies that were treated in this manner.

167

# Edible Flower Canapés

Edible flowers provide a striking palette with which to decorate food. With a small garden of edible flowers you can make your canapés look like edible art.

¹/₂ cup snipped fresh dill or chive leaves

1 pound natural cream cheese, softened

2 large loaves of dense sandwich or rustic-style unsliced bread, or 2 packages melba toast

A selection of edible flowers, 4 or 5 dozen: nasturtiums, borage, calendulas, pineapple sage, runner bean flowers, pansies, violas, violets, and mustard flowers

Herb leaves: sage, parsley, mint, dill, and basil

In a mixing bowl, add the chives and 3 tablespoons of water to the cream cheese and mix until smooth. If the mixture is too thick, add a little more water.

Trim the crusts off the bread and cut it into ¹/₃-inch-thick slices. Cut the slices into large squares or rectangles 2¹/₂ to 3¹/₂ inches wide. Spread the cream cheese mixture on the bread—approximately 1 tablespoon per square—and arrange the squares on cookie sheets. Cover them lightly with plastic wrap and refrigerate until ready to decorate.

Carefully wash the flowers and herbs and gently pat them dry on paper towels. Lay them out on damp paper towels and cover with plastic wrap. Refrigerate until ready to use, but not for more than a few hours.

Decorate each canapé square with an edible flower or two and an herb leaf or two. Re-cover the canapés lightly with plastic wrap and refrigerate until serving time. The canapés may be done a few hours in advance, but do not prepare them any earlier, or the garnishes will wilt.

Put a paper doily on a decorative tray, place decorated squares on the tray, and serve.

Appetizers for 6 to 8 people.

# Tulip and Endive Appetizer

If you can spare a few tulips in full bloom for an appetizer plate, you will set the party atwitter.

Inside leaves from 2 medium heads
of Bibb lettuce

4 or 5 large tulip flowers of
different colors

2 or 3 Belgian endives

**For the filling:**

4 ounces chèvre cheese

2 to 3 tablespoons heavy cream

Flavorings: minced pimiento strips;
finely chopped nasturtium or
violet petals; or minced fresh
herbs such as fennel, tarragon,
chives, and sorrel

Arrange a bed of Bibb lettuce leaves on a large serving platter.

Remove the petals from the tulips and gently wash them. Place them on paper towels to dry. Cut the root end off the endives and separate the leaves. Cover and refrigerate the lettuce, tulip petals, and endives if you're not serving them right away.

**To make the filling:** In a small bowl, use a fork to break up the chèvre, working in a few tablespoons of cream. Use enough cream to make the chèvre workable. With a fork, incorporate the flavorings to taste.

**To assemble the appetizers:** Lay out about 18 endive leaves. Top them with 1 or 2 tulip petals. At the base of each petal, place $^1/_2$ teaspoon or so of the chèvre mixture. Arrange the appetizers on the bed of Bibb lettuce and serve.

Makes 18 to 24.

# Pineapple Sage Salsa

Cathy Barash, executive garden editor of Meredith Books, created this recipe while visiting when my pineapple sage was in bloom. This salsa is a delicious accompaniment to fish, such as grilled swordfish or tuna, or serve it on a bed of baby greens as an appetizer.

- 1 pineapple, peeled, cored, and cut into small bite-size chunks
- 1 sweet yellow bell pepper, finely diced (about 1 cup)
- $^1/_2$ cup Vidalia or Walla Walla onion, finely chopped
- 2 tablespoons Rose's sweetened lime juice
- $^1/_2$ teaspoon ground dried ancho or other mild chile pepper
- $^1/_2$ cup pineapple sage flowers, measured, then coarsely chopped

In a glass or stainless-steel (nonreactive) bowl, toss together all the ingredi-

# Citrus Dip for Begonia Blossoms

The slightly crisp texture and sweet citrus flavor of begonias can be a spectacular ice-breaking appetizer. The blossoms come in many splashy colors, and a platterful makes a lovely centerpiece for a buffet table.

- 1 tablespoon honey
- 1 tablespoon frozen orange juice concentrate
- 1 teaspoon orange zest
- $^1/_2$ teaspoon lemon zest
- $^1/_2$ cup nonfat yogurt
- 4 large organically grown tuberous begonia flowers

In a small bowl, combine the honey, orange juice concentrate, and orange and lemon zests. Add the yogurt and mix well. Pour the yogurt mixture into a small, decorative bowl, cover it with plastic wrap, and refrigerate until ready to serve.

Just before serving, gently wash the begonia blossoms and remove each of the petals at its base. Place the bowl of flavored yogurt on a large platter and arrange the petals in a decorative pattern around the bowl. Serve the appetizer within the hour to prevent the petals from wilting.

Serves 4 to 6.

ents. Cover and refrigerate for at least 6 hours to allow the flavors to meld.

Makes about 2 cups.

# Ricotta-Stuffed Zucchini Flowers

This recipe was created by Vicki Sebastiani, famous for her garden, her cooking, and her family winery, Viansa Winery and Italian Marketplace in Sonoma, California. The proportions vary according to the number and sizes of the flowers. A word of caution: sometimes bees get trapped in the squash flowers.

1 pound ricotta cheese

1 onion, minced

$^1/_2$ cup toasted almonds, or pine nuts, finely chopped

$^1/_2$ cup grated Asiago (or Parmesan) cheese

$^1/_2$ teaspoon freshly ground black pepper

1 teaspoon seasoned salt

2 tablespoons minced fresh basil

2 tablespoons minced fresh Italian parsley

1 teaspoon melted butter

Approximately 20 to 30 medium zucchini (or any other squash) flowers, freshly picked

Garnish: nasturtium flowers

Rinse the flowers. Mix together all the ingredients except the butter and flowers. With the filling at room temperature, use a pastry tube to carefully stuff the flowers; do not overfill them.

Drizzle the melted butter over the flowers and microwave them on medium power for 3 minutes, or bake at 350°F in a regular oven for 15 minutes. Be careful not to overcook the flowers or allow the filling to ooze out.

Arrange the stuffed flowers on a serving platter. Garnish with nasturtiums stuffed with leftover filling.

Serves 10 as an appetizer.

# Sage Tempura

Ron Ottobre developed this flashy and incredibly tasty appetizer while he was executive chef at Mudd's Restaurant in San Ramon, California.

$^2/_3$ cup cornmeal

2 cups unbleached flour

4 tablespoons cornstarch

2 tablespoons baking powder

2 tablespoons sugar

2 teaspoons salt

$^1/_2$ cup whole milk

2 eggs, beaten

2 tablespoons peanut oil

Oil for frying

16 (4-inch) lengths of sage in bloom (flowers and leaves)

In a large bowl, sift together the cornmeal, flour, cornstarch, baking powder, sugar, and salt. In a separate bowl, whisk together 1 cup of water, the milk, eggs, and peanut oil. Gradually whisk together the two mixtures. In a heavy frying pan, heat about 1 inch of oil until a dollop of batter dropped in sizzles and bubbles. Dip the sage into the batter and drop into the oil (depending on the size of the frying pan, you can usually cook about 6 at a time without cooling down the oil too much). When they're lightly browned on one side, turn the sage over, and cook the other side. Remove to paper towels or brown paper to drain. Serve immediately with your favorite dipping sauce, or reheat in the oven the next day.

Serves 4.

**For the dressing:**

- 2 tablespoons rice-wine or
  champagne vinegar
- Salt and freshly ground black
  pepper
- 1 teaspoon frozen white grape juice
  or apple juice concentrate
- 3 or 4 tablespoons extra-virgin
  olive oil

**To make the salad:** Wash the lettuce and baby greens and dry them in a salad spinner or gently pat them dry with paper towels. In a large salad bowl, break the lettuce leaves into bite-size pieces and add baby greens. If not serving immediately, cover the bowl lightly with plastic wrap and refrigerate.

**To make the dressing:** In a small bowl, combine the vinegar, salt, pepper, and juice concentrate. Whisk in the oil until blended.

Wash the flowers gently, lightly pat them dry with paper towels, and gently pull off the petals. In a small bowl, stir the petals to mix the colors and make a confetti. You should have about ¹/₃ cup of loosely packed petals.

Stir the dressing, pour 3 or 4 tablespoons over the lettuce and greens, and toss. Add more dressing if needed, but be careful not to overwhelm the salad. Divide the salad equally among four salad plates. Scatter a small handful of flower-petal confetti over each individual salad and serve.

Serves 4.

# Flower Confetti Salad

Chartreuse butter lettuces and the warm colors of flower petals can dress up an everyday salad or start off a festive meal. A salad can be especially dramatic when prepared at the table. Pick flowers as close to serving time as possible. Put the stems in a glass of water and refrigerate.

**For the salad:**

- 1 large, or 2 small, heads of Bibb
  lettuce
- 1 large handful of mixed baby
  greens
- 6 to 8 edible flowers such as
  nasturtiums, calendulas, violas,
  pansies, rose petals, or
  chrysanthemums

# Wild Violet Salad

Violets are tasty and very nutritious and grow so easily they can become a pest. But what a pest. My violets give me greens and flowers from February to May. Look your garden over and see what other unusual greens can be harvested: pea shoots from edible peas, miner's lettuce, chickweed, or tiny young dandelion leaves.

**Caution:** Make sure you can positively identify your greens and that none have been sprayed with toxic chemicals.

**For the salad:**

- 1 large handful of baby mesclun greens
- 1 handful of young violet leaves
- 1 small head of romaine or butter lettuce
- 6 or 8 pea tendrils (tender shoots at the ends of the vines)
- 8 to 10 violet flowers

**For the dressing:**

- 1½ to 2 tablespoons balsamic or red wine vinegar
- 1 teaspoon honey
- Salt and freshly ground black pepper
- 2 tablespoons extra-virgin olive oil
- 1 tablespoon hazelnut or almond oil

Wash the mesclun greens, violet leaves, lettuces, and pea tendrils well in a large amount of water in the sink or in the bowl of a salad spinner. Vigorously slosh the greens up and down. Repeat the process two or three times until the water is completely clear. Spin the greens in the salad spinner or pat them dry with paper towels. Break the lettuce leaves and pea tendrils into bite-size pieces. Put the mesclun, lettuce, violet leaves, and pea tendrils in a salad bowl, cover, and refrigerate until serving time. Gently wash the flowers. Refrigerate in a glass of water until just before serving.

**To make the dressing:** In a small container, combine the vinegar, honey, salt, and pepper and with a fork or wire whisk blend in the oils. Drizzle the dressing over the greens and toss. Remove the stems from the flowers, add the flowers to the salad, and serve. Serves 4.

# Baby-Shower Petal Salad

This salad can be expanded to feed a large crowd. Plan on one large handful of salad greens per person and approximately ½ cup of dressing for six people. This is a great vehicle for showing off your garden, so include unusual greens like orach, ornamental cabbages, and violet leaves, as well as herbs like chervil and borage. Choose edible flowers in the pink, blue, and white range for a garnish.

**For the salad:**

6 handfuls of mixed salad greens

1 handful of baby leaves of fancy greens: orach, violets, ornamental cabbage, mizuna, tatsoi, amaranth, and mâche

6 to 8 large colorful ornamental cabbage leaves

**For the dressing:**

2 to 3 tablespoons champagne vinegar or white-wine vinegar

Salt and freshly ground black pepper

1 small garlic clove, finely minced (optional)

4 or 5 tablespoons extra-virgin olive oil

1 tablespoon finely chopped fresh mint or basil

Garnish: baby rose petals; straw-
berry blossoms; borage; violas; pansies; violets; dianthus; apple, pear, and plum blossoms; and chives

Wash the greens well, dry them in a salad spinner, and arrange them in a large bowl. Place the large leaves of ornamental cabbage around the out-side of the bowl.

In a small bowl, combine the vine-gar, salt, pepper, and garlic if desired. Whisk in the oil. Add the herbs and stir.

Just before serving, sprinkle the dressing over the greens. Arrange the flowers over the salad and serve imme-diately.

Serves 6.

# Mardi Gras Salad with Pecans

For an exciting winter dish, try a salad celebrating Mardi Gras. In New Orleans, the colors of Mardi Gras are gold, green, and blue. Since salad greens and cool-season edible flowers are at their best in mild climates during this February festival, a salad made with fresh greens at their peak and edible flowers in colors to match the theme is a real show-off dish and adds style to the celebration.

**For the dressing:**

3 tablespoons balsamic vinegar

Salt and freshly ground black pepper

5 tablespoons extra-virgin olive oil

1 to 2 tablespoons minced fresh lemon thyme or spearmint

1 small garlic clove, pressed

**For the salad:**

1 head butter lettuce

1/2 head of romaine

1 handful of fresh baby spinach leaves, or mature spinach broken into bite-size pieces

1/2 cup whole pecans

12 to 20 gold nasturtiums and calendulas, and blue and gold pansies and violas

**To make the dressing:** In a small bowl, combine the vinegar, salt, and pepper, blend in the oil, and add the thyme and garlic.

**To make the salad:** Wash the greens and break them into bite-size pieces. Place the greens and pecans in a large salad bowl.

Gently wash the flowers. Remove the petals and put them in a small bowl.

To serve, whisk the vinaigrette well, pour it over the greens, and toss gently. Adjust seasonings if necessary after the dressing is tossed with the greens. Just before serving, sprinkle flower petals over the salad.

Serves 4 to 6.

# Poor-Man's Pilaf

The perfume of the spices and the beauty of the flower petals makes this a special dish. To obtain the most color from the petals, mince the petals well before adding them to the rice. Serve with a salad for a light supper or as an interesting side dish.

About 15 cardamom pods

$^1/_8$ teaspoon cumin seeds

$^1/_8$ teaspoon coriander seeds

2 tablespoons vegetable oil

1 large onion, finely chopped

$1^1/_2$ cups basmati rice

1-inch-diameter sheaf of spaghetti, broken into 3-inch pieces

$3^1/_2$ cups homemade or low-sodium chicken stock or vegetable stock

1 cup cubed carrots

$^3/_4$ cup plus 2 tablespoons calendula petals, divided

$^1/_2$ teaspoon ground red pepper

1 cup fresh or frozen petit pois

$^1/_2$ cup sliced almonds

2 tablespoons safflower petals

Remove the outer shell of the cardamom pods and take out the seeds. (You need $^1/_8$ teaspoon.) In a dry sauté pan, toast the cardamom, cumin, and coriander seeds over low heat until they start to perfume the air. Remove them from the pan and grind them with a mortar and pestle or in a spice grinder. (I use a coffee grinder that I keep just for spices.) Set the spice mixture aside.

In a large sauté pan with a lid, heat the oil, and over medium-low heat sauté the onion until translucent, about 7 minutes. Add the rice and spaghetti and sauté over low heat until they start to brown. Add the chicken stock and the carrots to the pan carefully, as the oil may splatter. Chop $^3/_4$ cup of the ca-

lendula petals and add them to the rice mixture. Add the spice mixture and the pepper to the rice and stir. Cover and simmer on low heat for about 20 to 25 minutes, until the rice is tender and the liquid has been absorbed. Add the peas and cook until done, 1 or 2 more minutes. Take the pan off the

heat, stir in the almonds, and transfer to a serving bowl. Sprinkle on the safflower petals and the remaining 2 tablespoons calendula petals and serve.

Serves 4 to 6.

# Stir-Fried Beef with Anise Hyssop

This simple and delicious dish from Renee Shepherd, of Renee's Garden, uses anise hyssop to add a subtle flavor that enhances all the other ingredients. Serve over fluffy white rice.

> 1/2 cup chopped anise hyssop
>     flowers and leaves
> 1/3 cup soy sauce
> 1 tablespoon brown sugar
> 2 tablespoons sherry
> 1 pound flank steak, cut across the
>     grain into strips 3 inches long
>     and 1/4 inch wide
> 2 tablespoons vegetable oil
> 3 tablespoons chopped scallions
> 1/4 cup chicken broth
> 2 teaspoons cornstarch dissolved in
>     2 teaspoons water

In a bowl, combine the anise hyssop flowers and leaves, soy sauce, brown sugar, and sherry. Pour the mixture over the steak strips and marinate for several hours.

Remove the meat from the marinade, reserving the remaining sauce. In a wok or large skillet, heat the oil and stir-fry the meat quickly over medium-high heat until brown, about 5 minutes. Add the scallions, the chicken broth, and the marinade and heat through. Stir in the cornstarch mixture until the sauce thickens. Garnish with flowers if desired.

Serves 4 to 6.

# Rose Petal Syrup

This versatile syrup can be used on crepes or pancakes, drizzled over sponge cake, or used in sorbets. My favorite roses to use are 'Belle of Portugal,' 'Abraham Darby,' and the spicy *Rosa rugosa alba*. Try your own varieties for flavor. Some are sensational, others metallic or bitter tasting. If the white bases of the petals are bitter, remove them.

**Caution:** Use only roses that have not been sprayed with commercial chemicals. Diners allergic to sulfur should be particularly careful, as organic gardeners often use sulfur to control rose diseases.

2 cups rose petals

$^2/_3$ cup sugar

Wash the petals and dry them in a salad spinner. Check for insects. Chop the petals very fine. In a medium saucepan, bring 1 cup of water to a boil and stir in the sugar. When the sugar is melted, add the petals. Remove the syrup from the heat and cover it tightly. Let it steep overnight.

Taste the syrup the next day, and if the flavor is not strong enough, reheat the syrup, add more petals, and let it steep overnight again. You can store the syrup in the refrigerator for up to two weeks—freeze it for longer storage.

Makes 1 cup.

# Rose Petal Sorbet

Micheal Isles, chef/instructor in Chico, California, created this fabulous treat. Make the syrup at least two days before making the sorbet.

1 cup rose petal syrup (see page 86 for recipe)

1 bottle of late harvest Gewürztraminer grape juice

4 perfect, large rose blossoms

1 egg white

A day before serving, combine the syrup and grape juice in an ice cream maker. Follow the manufacturer's directions for making sorbet. Once the sorbet is done, freeze it in an airtight container for 24 hours. You can get away with only 3 hours as an absolute minimum.

To serve, choose four perfect, large roses, remove the centers, spread them open, and secure them to the middle of the plates or dishes with a little egg white. Just before serving, place a scoop of sorbet in each rose. The sorbet may also be served in sherbet glasses or floating in champagne in fancy long-stemmed goblets.

Serves 4 to 6.

# Lavender Ice Cream

This recipe was inspired by Chef David Schy when he was chef at the El Encanto Hotel in Santa Barbara. He served this ice cream at a seminar, and participants were reduced to bickering like children over who had the most.

14 ounces whole milk

1½ ounces fresh lavender flowers and leaves

2 ounces crystallized ginger, minced

1 cup granulated sugar

3 egg yolks

2 cups heavy whipping cream, cold

In a saucepan, slowly heat the milk to approximately 200°F. Remove from heat, add the lavender flowers, and steep for 15 minutes. While it's still warm, strain the milk through a cheesecloth. Add the ginger and sugar to the milk. Place the egg yolks in a small bowl and pour in half of the milk mixture. Stir the mixture with a spoon, then pour it back into the saucepan. Place the pan over low heat and cook until the mixture is approximately 200°F. Remove the saucepan from the heat and stir in the whipping cream. Refrigerate the mixture until it is well chilled, then process in any ice-cream machine.

Makes 1 quart.

# Tangelo and Kiwi Salad with Orange Blossoms

This citrus salad is lovely to look at, and the flavors are both familiar yet slightly different. Taste your citrus petals before adding them to the dressing. Expect some bitterness; but if they are very harsh, try blossoms from another tree. The point of adding a few citrus blossoms to the dressing is to infuse the tangelo juice with a lovely aroma and to deepen the citrus flavor.

6 medium tangelos, divided, or 3 tangelos and 1 cup of bottled fresh tangerine juice

1 tablespoon fresh lemon juice

5 lemon, tangerine, or orange blossoms, divided

1 tablespoon honey (optional)

2 kiwifruit

Squeeze 3 of the tangelos and put the juice (or the bottled tangerine juice) in a medium bowl. Add the lemon juice and the petals of 3 of the orange blossoms. If the tangelos are not very sweet, add a tablespoon of honey. Peel and section the remaining 3 tangelos, peel and slice the kiwifruit, add them to the juice mixture, and stir to cover the fruit. Refrigerate for a few hours.

To serve, divide the fruit among four serving dishes. Pour the tangelo juice over the fruit and garnish with the remaining citrus blossom petals.

Serves 4.

# Scented Geranium, Crème Fraîche, and Strawberries

Carole Saville, author of *Exotic Herbs*, has perfected cooking with scented geraniums—this is one of her recipes.

1 tablespoon finely minced rose-scented geranium leaves

3 tablespoons granulated sugar, divided

1 cup crème fraîche (see Note)

2 pints strawberries

Garnish: scented geranium flowers

In a small bowl, combine the scented geranium leaves, 2 tablespoons of sugar, and crème fraîche. Cover the bowl with plastic wrap and refrigerate for 48 hours. Scrape the crème fraîche into a large, fine-mesh sieve, and with the back of a spoon push it through and into another bowl. Discard the geranium leaves. Cover the crème fraîche with plastic wrap and return it to the refrigerator until ready to serve.

Wash and hull the strawberries. Cut large ones into slices. Sprinkle with remaining 1 tablespoon sugar. Divide the strawberries among four small glass cups or bowls. Spoon the scented crème fraîche over each serving. Garnish with scented geranium flowers.

Serves 4.

**Note:** Crème fraîche is readily available in France, but is still a bit expensive and hard to find here. A good approximation can easily be made at home.

Place 1 cup heavy cream and 1 tablespoon buttermilk in a small bowl. Stir well, cover the bowl with plastic wrap, and leave the mixture at room temperature until it thickens slightly, about 12 to 24 hours depending on the temperature. Once it is thickened, refrigerate the crème fraîche until you are ready to use it. It will keep in the refrigerator for about a week.

# Tea Cake with Anise Hyssop and Lemon

Another recipe from Renee Shepherd, this combination of anise and lemon will especially please those who do not like things too sweet. This cake keeps well and actually tastes best after being wrapped in foil overnight.

2 cups all-purpose flour

1 tablespoon baking powder

$1/2$ teaspoon salt

$1/2$ cup butter, room temperature

$1/2$ cup granulated sugar

Grated zest of 1 lemon

$1/3$ to $1/2$ cup anise hyssop flowers, finely chopped

2 eggs, beaten

$1/2$ cup fresh lemon juice

$1/2$ cup chopped walnuts

Grease and flour a bread or loaf pan. Heat the oven to 350°F.

Sift together the flour, baking powder, and salt. In another bowl, with a hand mixer cream the butter with the sugar until fluffy. Then add the lemon zest, flowers, and eggs and beat the mixture just until thoroughly combined. Stir in the lemon juice. Gradually mix in the flour mixture and walnuts, until blended. Spoon the mixture into the pan and bake for 50 to 55 minutes. Let the cake cool on a rack.

Makes 1 loaf.

# Lavender Shortbreads

Shortbread cookies lend themselves to all sorts of special flavor variations. Here, I use lavender, but rose geraniums would be tasty too. Shortbread cookie stamps are available from some specialty baking-supply houses.

2 cups unsalted butter, room temperature

1 cup "Lavender Sugar" (see recipe, page 71)

$1/2$ teaspoon salt

4 cups all-purpose flour

2 teaspoons dried lavender blossoms

**To make the shortbread:** Using the paddle attachment on a stand mixer, blend the butter, lavender sugar, and salt on a low to medium speed until light and fluffy, about 10 minutes. Work in the flour gradually, scraping the bowl occasionally to blend all the ingredients well. Mix in the lavender blossoms. Shape the dough into a ball, wrap it in plastic wrap, and refrigerate it for at least 2 hours.

**To shape the shortbread:** If you're using a cookie stamp, cut the dough into golf-ball-size pieces. Roll each piece into a ball with your floured hands, then press it with the lightly floured stamp. Gently remove the stamp and place the formed dough on a cookie sheet lined with parchment paper.

If you don't have a stamp, roll out the dough on a floured board to about $1/2$ inch thick. Using a cookie cutter or a 3-inch-diameter water glass, cut out circles and place them on a parchment-lined cookie sheet. Score each cookie

with the tines of a fork a few times, making a pleasing pattern. You can also cut the dough into equal rectangles instead of circles.

Refrigerate the formed cookies for 30 minutes before baking them.

Preheat the oven to 300°F. Bake the shortbread for 25 to 30 minutes, or until it is pale golden but not brown.

Makes about 2 dozen cookies.

# appendix A planting and maintenance

C overed in this section are the basics of soil preparation, starting seeds, transplanting, composting, mulching, watering and irrigation, and maintaining most annual, perennial, and woody, edible flowering plants and herbs.

## Soil Preparation

### Trees and Shrubs

This section covers pineapple guava, elderberry, redbud, lilac, lemon, orange, and apple trees. Since these plantings are permanent, you need to give a lot of thought to where you plant them. Will they get too large for the location? Is the soil in the area well drained? Is there enough sunlight in the chosen spot? Most woody plants need fast-draining soil and at least six hours of midday sun. Even though homeowners want to plant them in a lawn, they never grow very well surrounded by grass: they must compete for nutrients and water, are damaged by mowers and trimmers, and, if the lawn needs constant irrigation, they eventually develop a number of diseases.

Once you've decided on where to put your tree or shrub, it's time to plant. Woody plants are best planted in the spring when they are most available in nurseries and when they will have a long season to get established before winter cold sets in. Apple trees are available bare root, that is, when they are dormant and the roots are wrapped for protection, but without soil, or in containers. Other trees and shrubs are usually sold only in five-gallon containers.

To prepare the soil for your tree or shrub, dig a hole that is double the width of the root ball and six inches deeper. Mix in a cup or so of bonemeal around the bottom and rough up the sides of the hole with a spade or digging fork. Mix in half a wheelbarrowful of organic matter, but only if the soil is light and sandy. (Contrary to past recommendations to amend the planting hole in heavy soils with copious amounts of organic matter, we now know that the roots of woody plants seldom leave amended fluffy soil to venture out into dense native soils. Instead, they remain confined to the planting hole. When the soil is not amended, the roots extend far into the parent soil.) Examine the root ball.

Use a knife or sharp spade to cut through any thick mat of roots on the sides and bottom. Shovel some of the soil back in the hole and place the tree or shrub in the hole an inch or so higher than it was in the container. Straighten the roots out onto the backfill in the hole. Shovel the soil back in the hole and gently tamp the soil in place with your foot. Build up a small watering basin and water the plant in well by filling the basin full of water three or four times. Apply a mulch of organic matter at least three inches deep and at least six inches away from the trunk, to prevent the crown of the tree (where the bark meets the roots) from staying moist and possibly rotting. Keep the newly planted tree fairly moist for the first month and then start to taper off with the watering. In rainy climates, water the tree if it rains less than once a week. In arid climates, water deeply with at least one inch of water a week in hot weather. Drip irrigation is ideal for this purpose.

### Flowers

If you are planning a new garden area in which to plant annual and perennial flowers, plus a few vegetables, or you are installing a rose garden, the soil must be prepared more thoroughly. These plants need rich soil filled with organic matter and great drainage. To prepare the soil for a new garden, first remove large rocks and weeds. Dig out any perennial weeds and grasses, making sure to get out all the roots (including all those little pieces). It's tedious but will save you lots of work in the long run, as they usually come back—unfortunately up through your new plants. If you are taking up part of a lawn, the sod needs to be removed. If it is a small area, this can be done with a flat spade. Removing large sections, though, warrants renting a sod cutter. Next, when the soil is not too wet, spade over the area. Then cover it with three or four inches of compost (or other organic matter such as leaf mold or well-aged manure). Add even more compost if you live in a hot, humid climate where heat burns the compost at an accelerated rate, or if you have very alkaline, very sandy, or very heavy clay soil. Most plants grow best in a soil pH between 6 and 7, so add lime at this time if your soil is acidic, following the

## USDA Plant Hardiness Zone Map

| AVERAGE ANNUAL MINIMUM TEMPERATURE |||
| --- | --- | --- |
| Temperature (°C) | Zone | Temperature (°F) |
| -45.6 and Below | 1 | Below -50 |
| -42.8 to -45.5 | 2a | -45 to -50 |
| -40.0 to -42.7 | 2b | -40 to -45 |
| -37.3 to -40.0 | 3a | -35 to -40 |
| -34.5 to -37.2 | 3b | -30 to -35 |
| -31.7 to -34.4 | 4a | -25 to -30 |
| -28.9 to -31.6 | 4b | -20 to -25 |
| -26.2 to -28.8 | 5a | -15 to -20 |
| -23.4 to -26.1 | 5b | -10 to -15 |
| -20.6 to -23.3 | 6a | -5 to -10 |
| -17.8 to -20.5 | 6b | 0 to -5 |
| -15.0 to -17.7 | 7a | 5 to 0 |
| -12.3 to -15.0 | 7b | 10 to 5 |
| -9.5 to -12.2 | 8a | 15 to 10 |
| -6.7 to -9.4 | 8b | 20 to 15 |
| -3.9 to -6.6 | 9a | 25 to 20 |
| -1.2 to -3.8 | 9b | 30 to 25 |
| 1.6 to -1.1 | 10a | 35 to 30 |
| 4.4 to 1.7 | 10b | 40 to 35 |
| 4.5 and Above | 11 | 40 and Above |

The USDA Plant Hardiness Zone Map is most useful when you are growing perennial plants because it indicates how cold a given area will be during an average winter. In order to use the map, locate your geographical area and consult the color code that indicates which zone you are in. When you select plants for your garden, choose ones that grow in your zone. Remember, however, that the zone only indicates how cold your garden will get, but there are many other factors that affect the health of your plants, namely summer highs and your area's soil type.

directions on the package. Incorporate the ingredients thoroughly by turning over the soil with a spade. Add some bonemeal and work it into the top eight inches of soil, at the rate of 4 cups per 100 square feet. If your garden is large or the soil is very hard to work, you might use a rototiller to turn the soil. (When you put in a garden for the first time, a rototiller can be very helpful. However, research has shown that continued use of tillers is hard on soil structure and quickly burns up valuable organic matter if used regularly.) If you can do this soil preparation a few weeks before you plant, so much the better.

Finally, grade and rake the area. Make paths at least 3 feet wide through your garden so you can care for and harvest the flowers. Because of all the added materials, the beds will now be elevated above the paths—which further helps drainage. Slope the sides of the beds so that loose soil will not be washed or knocked onto the paths. Some gardeners add a brick or stone edging to outline the beds. Some sort of gravel, brick, stone, or mulch is needed on the paths to forestall weed growth, to give a strong design to your garden, and most important, to prevent your feet from getting wet and muddy.

Once the beds are prepared, it is planting time. I obtain my edible flower plants in different ways. Many of the annual flowers and vegetables I start from seeds. Plants like nasturtiums, calendulas, arugula, and marigolds are easily started from seeds, and radishes can be obtained no other way. Sometimes I buy my plants from nurseries if they have the varieties I want or if I'm late getting seeds started. Most perennials I purchase from local or mail-order nurseries, and plants that divide easily like chives and daylilies I usually get as divisions from a neighbor's plant. I find starting from seeds gives me lots of options with many fun varieties. Whereas the local nursery might carry one or two varieties of nasturtiums or calendulas, I might find a dozen varieties in a mail-order catalog.

## Herbs

To prepare the soil for a new garden of herbs, first remove large rocks and weeds. Dig out any perennial weeds and grasses,

making sure to get out all the roots, or they will come back and, unfortunately, up through your new herb plants. If you are taking up part of a lawn, the sod will need to be removed. If it is a small area, this can be done with a flat spade. Removing large sections, though, warrants renting a sod cutter. Next, when the soil is not too wet, spade over the area. If you are going to be planting many annual herbs and may be adding salad greens, vegetables, and annual flowers, you need to supplement your soil with a lot of organic matter and an organic nitrogen fertilizer, as most soil is deficient in these materials. Very sandy soil also needs a lot of added organic matter to help hold moisture and fertility. A garden of mostly perennial herbs, though, in average soil needs no added fertilizer, except some bonemeal worked into the top eight inches of soil before planting, at the rate of 4 cups per 100 square feet. After the area has been spaded up, cover it with four or five inches of compost and an inch or two of well-aged manure. Add even more compost if you live in a hot, humid climate where heat burns the compost at an accelerated rate, or if you have very alkaline, very sandy, or very heavy clay soil. Since most herbs grow best in a neutral soil, add lime at this point if your soil is acidic. Follow the directions on the package. If you are planting a number of annual herbs or adding vegetables and annual flowers, sprinkle fish fertilizer or chicken manure over the beds where they are to be planted. Incorporate the ingredients thoroughly by turning the soil over with a spade. If your garden is large or the soil is very hard to work, you might use a rototiller. (When you put in a garden for the first time, sometimes one is needed. However, research has shown that continued use of tillers is hard on soil structure and quickly burns up valuable organic matter if used regularly.) If you can do this

### To Divide Perennial Herbs

Use a sharp spade to cut down through the middle of the clump (*top*). Lift the clump out of the ground (*middle*). Once the herb is out of the ground cut the clump in three or four pieces with a spade (*bottom*). Each piece is now a new plant and can be given its own planting hole. Cut the divided plants back by at least half and water them in.

soil preparation a few weeks before you plant, so much the better.

Finally, grade and rake the area. You are now ready to form the beds and paths. Because of all the added materials, the beds will now be elevated above the paths—which further helps drainage. Slope the beds away from the paths so loose soil will not be washed or knocked onto the paths. Some gardeners add a brick or stone edging to outline the beds. Some sort of gravel, brick, stone, or mulch is needed on the paths to prevent weeds, to give a strong design to your garden, and, most important, to prevent your feet from getting wet and muddy. Once paths are in place, lay out plants where they are to be planted. Choose short species for the front of the beds and tall ones for the rear. Step back and see how you like the color contrast of foliage and flower you have chosen, then fine-tune your design. Also refresh your memory as to how far the plants will spread, so they won't be crowded once they mature. Few gardeners get it right the first time, however. I always make a few mistakes and end up moving herbs around as the design comes together. That's half the fun.

One last possible step to consider for herb gardens in cool-summer areas or in hot, humid climates is that of applying a pebble mulch. In cool-summer gardens they provide extra heat to the plant by absorbing it in the day and releasing it back at night. I visited Madalene Hill and Gwen Barclay in hot, humid Texas, and they find that a two-inch gravel mulch helps provide a cool root zone and gives fast drainage, both of which help prevent fungus problems for drought-tolerant herbs. Before installing them, clear the ground of weeds, especially perennial ones, as removing the gravel mulch to replant is a daunting project. To make sure weeds don't come up through any type of mulch, some gardeners report success by placing six to eight layers of damp black-and-white newspaper sheets down before adding the gravel.

## Starting from Seeds

You can grow most annual and many perennial edible flowers or herbs from seeds. They can be started indoors in flats or other well-drained containers or outdoors in a cold frame, or with some easily started annuals like nasturtiums and calendulas, directly in the garden. Starting seeds inside is usually preferable, as it gives your seedlings a warm and safe start.

The cultural needs of seeds vary widely among species. Still, some basic rules apply to most seeding procedures. First, whether you are starting seeds in the ground or in a container, make sure you have a loose, water-retentive soil that drains well. Good drainage is important because seeds can get waterlogged, and too much water can lead to "damping off," a fungal disease that kills seedlings at the soil line. Commercial starting mixes are usually best since they have been sterilized to remove weed seeds; however, the quality varies greatly from brand to brand, and I find most lack enough nitrogen, so I water with a weak solution of fish emulsion when I plant the seeds, and again every few weeks.

Smooth the soil surface and plant the seeds at the recommended depth. Pat down the seeds, and water carefully to make the seed bed moist but not soggy. When starting seeds outside, protect the seedbed with bird netting to keep out critters. If slugs and snails are a problem, circle the area with diatomaceous earth to keep them away, and go out at night with a flashlight to catch any that cross the barrier. If you are starting edible flowers in containers, put the seedling tray in a warm place to help seeds germinate more quickly.

When starting seeds inside, once they have germinated it's imperative that they immediately be given a quality source of light. A greenhouse, sunporch, greenhouse window, or south-facing window with no overhang will suffice, provided that it is warm. If one is not available, use fluorescent lights, which are available from home-supply stores or from specialty mail-order houses.

Keep the soil moist and, if you have seeded thickly and have crowded plants, thin the seedlings. It's less damaging to do so with small scissors. Cut the little plants out, leaving the remaining seedlings an inch or so apart. Do not transplant your seedlings until they have their second set of true leaves (the first leaves that sprout from a seed are called seed leaves and usually look different from the later true leaves). If the seedlings are tender, wait until all danger of frost is past before you set them out. Young plants started indoors or in a greenhouse should be "hardened off" before they are planted in the garden—that is, they should be put outside in a sheltered place for a few days in their containers to let them get used to the differences in temperature, humidity, and air movement.

## Transplanting

Before setting out transplants in the garden, check to see if a mat of roots has formed at the bottom of the root ball. I open it up so the roots won't continue to grow in a tangled mass. Even though the garden bed has been well prepared and by this time lots of organic matter and bonemeal have been added, for the heavy-feeding broccoli, mustard, and squash, I supplement the planting area with some form of nitrogen fertilizer. I add either fish meal, following the prescribed amount given on the package, or a few shovels full of chicken manure for each plant. I then set the plant in the ground at the same height as it was in the container if it's a 4-inch container or smaller, and a little above ground level if it's in a one-gallon container or larger. I pat the plant in place gently by hand, and water each plant in well to remove air bubbles. If I'm planting on a very hot day or the transplants have been in a protected greenhouse, I shade them with a shingle or such, placed on the sunny side of the plants. I then install my drip irrigation tubing at this time (see "Watering and Irrigation Systems") and then mulch with a few inches of organic matter. I keep the transplants moist but not soggy for the first few weeks.

## Mulching

Mulching with organic matter can save the gardener time, effort, and water, and the process builds great soil. A mulch reduces moisture loss, prevents erosion, controls weeds, minimizes soil compaction, and moderates soil temperature—keeping the roots cool in the summer and preventing them from heaving out of the soil in the winter. The organic material adds nutrients and organic matter to the soil as it decom-poses, and it helps keep heavy clay porous and helps sandy soils retain moisture. Applying a few inches of organic matter every spring is necessary in most garden beds to keep them healthy. Mulch with compost from your compost pile, pine nee-dles, composted sawdust, straw, or one of the many agricultural by-products such as rice hulls or grape pomace.

## Composting

Compost is the humus-rich result of the decomposition of organic matter, such as leaves and lawn clippings. The objective in maintaining a composting system is to speed up decomposition and centralize the material so you can gather it up and spread it where it will do the most good. Compost's benefits include providing nutri-ents to plants in a slow-release, balanced fashion; helping break up clay soil; aiding sandy soil to retain moisture; and correct-ing pH problems. On top of that, compost is free, it can be made at home, and it is an excellent way to recycle our yard and kitchen wastes. Compost can be used as a soil additive or a mulch.

There need be no great mystique about composting. To create the environment needed by the decay-causing microorgan-isms that do all the work, just include the following four ingredients, mixed well: three or four parts "brown" material high in carbon, such as dry leaves, dry grass, or even shredded black-and-white newspaper; one part "green" material high in nitrogen, such as fresh grass clippings, fresh garden trimmings, barnyard manure, or kitchen trimmings like pea pods and carrot tops; water in moderate amounts, so that the mixture is moist but not soggy; and air to supply oxygen to the microorganisms. Bury the kitchen trimmings within the pile, so as not to attract flies. Cut up any large pieces of material. Exclude weeds that have gone to seed, ivy clippings, and Bermuda grass clippings, because they can lead to the growth of those weeds, ivy, and Bermuda grass in the garden. Do not add meat, fat, diseased plants, woody branches, or cat or dog manure.

I don't stress myself about the proper

A three-bin composting system

proportions of compost materials, as long as I have a fairly good mix of materials from the garden. If the decomposition is too slow, it is usually because the pile has too much brown material, is too dry, or needs air. If the pile smells, there is too much green material or it is too wet. To speed up decomposition, I often chop or shred the materials before adding them to the pile and I may turn the pile occasionally to get additional oxygen to all parts. During decomposition, the materials can become quite hot and steamy, which is great; how-ever, it is not mandatory that the compost become extremely hot.

You can make compost in a simple pile, wire or wood bins, or in rather expensive containers. The size should be about three feet high, wide, and tall for the most effi-cient decomposition and so the pile is easily workable. It can be up to five feet by five feet, but it then becomes harder to manage. In a rainy climate, it's a good idea to have a cover for the compost. I like to use three bins. I collect the compost materials in one bin, have a working bin, and when that bin is full, I turn the contents into the last bin, where it finishes its decomposition. I sift the finished compost into empty garbage cans so it does not leach its nutrients into the soil. The empty bin is then ready to fill up again.

## Watering and Irrigation Systems

Even gardeners who live in rainy climates may need to do supplemental watering at

specific times during the growing season. Therefore, most gardeners need some sort of supplemental watering system and a knowledge of water management.

There is no easy formula for determin-ing the correct amount or frequency of watering. Proper watering takes experience and observation. In addition to the specific watering needs noted above, the water needs of a particular plant depend on soil type, wind conditions, air temperature, and the type of plant. To water properly, you must learn how to recognize water-stress symptoms (often a dulling of foliage color as well as the better-known symptoms of drooping leaves and wilting), how much to water (too much is as bad as too little), and how to water. Some general rules are

1. Water deeply. Except for seed beds, most plants need infrequent deep watering rather than frequent light sprinkling.

2. To ensure proper absorption, apply water at a rate slow enough to prevent runoff.

3. Do not use overhead watering systems when the wind is blowing.

4. Try to water early in the morning so that foliage will have time to dry off before nightfall, thus preventing some disease problems. In addition, because of the cooler temperature, less water is lost to evaporation.

5. Test your watering system occasionally to make sure it is covering the area evenly.

6. Use methods and tools that conserve water. When you are using a hose, a pistol-grip nozzle will shut off the water while you move from one container or planting

Baby lettuces with drip irrigation

bed to another. Soaker hoses, made of either canvas or recycled tires, and other ooze and drip irrigation systems apply water slowly to shrub borders and vegetable gardens and use water more efficiently than do overhead systems.

Drip, or the related ooze/trickle, irrigation systems are advisable wherever feasible, and most gardens are well suited to them. Drip systems deliver water a drop at a time through spaghetti-like emitter tubes or plastic pipe with emitters, that drip water right onto the root zone of each plant. Because of the time and effort involved in installing one or two emitters per plant, these systems work best for permanent plantings such as in rose beds, with rows of daylilies and lavender, say, or with trees and shrubs. These lines require continual maintenance to make sure the individual emitters are not clogged.

Other similar systems, called ooze systems, deliver water through either holes made every 6 or 12 inches along solid flexible tubing or ooze along the entire porous hose. Neither system is as prone to clogging as are the emitters. The solid type is made of plastic and is often called laser tubing. It is pressure compensated, which means the flow of water is even throughout the length of the tubing. The high-quality brands have a built-in mechanism to minimize clogging and are made of tubing that will not expand in hot weather and, consequently, pop off their fittings. (Some of the

inexpensive drip irrigation kits can make you crazy!) The porous-hose types are made from recycled tires and come in two sizes—a standard hose diameter of one inch, great for shrubs and trees planted in a row, and $1/4$-inch tubing that can be snaked around beds of small plants. Neither are pressure compensated, which means the plants nearest the source of water get more water than those at the end of the line. It also means they will not work well if there is any slope. All types of drip emitter and ooze systems are installed after the plants are in the ground, and are held in place with ground staples.

To install any drip or ooze systems, you must also install an anti-siphon valve at the water sources to prevent dirty garden water from being drawn up into the house drinking water. Further, a filter is also needed to prevent debris from clogging the filters. One-inch distribution tubing is connected to the water source and laid out around the perimeter of the garden. Then smaller-diameter drip and ooze lines are connected to this. As you can see, installing these systems requires some thought and time. You can order these systems from either a specialty mail-order garden or irrigation source or visit your local plumbing-supply store. I find the latter to be the best solution for all my irrigation problems. Over the years, I've found that plumbing-supply stores offer professional-quality supplies, usually for less money than the so-called

inexpensive kits available in home-supply stores and some nurseries. In addition to quality materials, there are professionals there to help you lay out an irrigation design that is tailored to your garden. Whether you choose an emitter or an ooze system, when you go to buy your tubing, be prepared by bringing a rough drawing of the area to be irrigated—with dimensions, the location of the water source and any slopes, and, if possible, the water pressure at your water source. Let the professionals walk you through the steps and help pick out supplies that best fit your site.

Problems aside, all forms of drip irrigation are more efficient than furrow or standard overhead watering in delivering water to its precise destination, and they are well worth considering. They deliver water slowly, so it doesn't run off; they also water deeply, which encourages deep rooting. Drip irrigation also eliminates many disease problems, and because so little of the soil surface is moist, there are fewer weeds. Finally, they have the potential to waste a lot less water.

## Maintaining the Edible Garden

The backbone of appropriate maintenance is a knowledge of your soil and weather, an ability to recognize basic water- and nutrient-deficiency symptoms, and a familiarity with the plants you grow.

### Annual Herbs

Annual herbs are growing machines. As a rule, they need to grow rapidly and with few interruptions so they will produce succulent leaves and have few pest problems. Once the plants are in the ground, continual monitoring for nutrient deficiencies or drought can head off problems. Keep the beds weeded; weeds compete for moisture and nutrients. In normal soil, dill, cilantro, and chervil will not need fertilizer, but basil will probably need a light application of a nitrogen fertilizer such as fish emulsion or fish meal midseason if it is to produce heavily.

## Perennial Herbs

As a rule, once perennial herbs are established, they require less routine maintenance than most flowers and vegetables. Fertilizing is not needed for average soil, and pests and diseases are much less a problem than with vegetables and many flowers. There is a short section on pests and diseases in Appendix B; the major tasks needed for herb gardening—annual pruning, weeding, and mulching—are addressed here.

## Weeding Herbs

Weeding is needed to make sure unwanted plants don't compete with and overpower your herbs. Be especially vigilant and look for perennial grasses, which if left in place will grow among and over perennial herbs and obliterate them. A good small triangular hoe will help you weed a small area of herbs if you start when the plants are small and easily pulled. If you allow the weeds to get large, then a session of hand pulling will be needed. In all herb plantings, if you apply a good mulch every spring, the need to weed will be minimal after a few years as the herb plants fill in and the annual mulch prevents seeds from sprouting.

## Pruning Herbs

Even if you plant your herbs in an informal design, all perennial herbs need occasional pruning. As a rule, a major pruning is needed every spring to force the plants to produce new succulent growth, to keep them from overgrowing an area, and to remove winter damage in cold climates. If you will be harvesting the herbs regularly throughout the growing season, many of the plants will need no further pruning. If you will not be harvesting the herbs in any significant way, and especially in long, mild climates, further pruning midseason after flowering is recommended to prevent the plants from getting woody and sometimes splaying in the middle. I find with herbs growing in my Zone 9 garden that regular light prunings work better than an occasional severe pruning. Basil needs continual harvesting or pruning, or the seed heads develop and the plant yields few leaves for harvesting. Start pruning when the plant is six inches tall and keep pinching back new growth and removing the flower spikes. Eventually, though, the plant will probably get ahead of you, so be ready for a major harvest or a pruning with hedge clippers.

## Annual Flowers

Annual plants are growing machines. As a rule, they need to grow rapidly with few interruptions so they have few pest problems. Once the plants are in the ground, continually monitoring them for nutrient deficiencies or drought can head off problems. Keep the beds weeded because the weeds compete for moisture and nutrients. In normal soil, anise hyssop, bee balm, borage, chives, saffron crocus, arugula, calendulas, dill, cilantro, fennel, violets, and nasturtiums usually will not need fertilizer, but broccoli, mustards, squash, strawberries, marigolds, violas, and pansies usually need a light application of a nitrogen fertilizer such as fish emulsion or fish meal midseason if they are to grow well. Pruning is seldom needed, but removing spent flowers, called deadheading, will cause most to flower more heavily and give the plants a neater appearance.

## Perennial Flowers

As a rule, once perennials are established, they require less routine maintenance than most annuals. Fertilizing is usually not needed for average soil that has been well prepared (though most will benefit from an inch or two of compost applied once or twice a year). Pests and diseases are much less a problem than with annuals. The major tasks for perennials are weeding, annual pruning, and mulching and winter protection in cold climates.

You need to weed to make sure unwanted plants don't compete with and overpower your plants. Be especially vigilant and look for perennial grasses, which if left in place will grow among and over perennials like lavender, daylilies, saffron crocus, pinks, and strawberries and obliterate them. A good, small, triangular hoe will help you weed a small area if you start when the weeds are small and easily pulled. If you allow the weeds to get large, then a session of hand pulling is needed. In perennial plantings, if you apply a good mulch every spring, the need to weed will be minimal after a few years as the plants fill in and the annual mulch prevents weed seeds from sprouting.

Many perennials, like lavender, rosemary, sage, and thyme, need a major pruning every spring to force them to produce new succulent growth, to keep them from overgrowing an area, and to remove winter damage in cold climates. In long-season, mild climates, further pruning midseason after flowering is recommended to prevent the plants from getting woody and sometimes splaying in the middle. Chrysanthemums need pruning in late spring and again in early summer to keep them bushy and to prevent splaying. Other perennials such as anise hyssop, bee balm, pinks, and daylilies need pruning after they bloom to remove spent flower heads and to look neat and tidy.

The less hardy perennials need winter protection in the coldest climates. In the fall, after the ground has frozen, apply a six- to eight-inch mulch of straw or composted material around the plants to insulate the soil and prevent the cycle of freezing and thawing that heaves plants out of the ground. It also prevents the plants from drying out in cold, dry weather when there is not enough snow to cover the plants. Some plants can be grown in containers and brought inside to a cool, dry place and then taken back out to the garden after the weather warms up.

## Trees and Shrubs

The maintenance of trees and shrubs differs for each species. See the information in the "Encyclopedia of Edible Flowers" for specific information; only the generalities are covered here. Woody plants need the most care in the first five years, when they are getting established. Young trees will need pruning to give them a well-formed shape; depending on the species, they may need pruning for optimum fruit production. They also need protection from cold in winter if they are tender, weeds removed from under the canopy of the tree, and an annual application of a well-balanced fertilizer such as fish meal or chicken manure in the spring. Throughout their lifetime they will grow best with a spring mulch, weed removal, and supplemental water during periods of drought.

## Selecting and Planting Roses

Variety selection is critical when choosing roses for your garden. Select those that are the most resistant to the diseases that are prevalent in your area. Try to resist being enticed by those photos of gorgeous roses—they will not look gorgeous when they are covered with diseases. And you will not be able to eat the flowers if they are covered with toxic fungicides. Contact the American Rose Society, your local rose society, county agricultural extension agent, or locally owned nurseries for information on roses that are suitable for your area. Unfortunately, it is difficult to get roses tailored to your climate from large chain nurseries and building-supply firms, as they often offer the same roses nationwide. As a rule, some of the old varieties and most modern shrub landscape roses have far fewer problems than most hybrid tea and floribunda roses.

When you are planting roses, calculate how far each variety will spread and how tall it will get. Situate the short varieties in the front of the bed and the tall ones in back. Fungus diseases are the major problem when you grow roses, so it's critical that you give each plant plenty of room for good air circulation. (Note that the planting size for roses listed in catalogs is an average. If you live in the coldest part of a recommended zone for a particular rose, assume that the plant will be smaller than described. If you live in a mild-winter area, assume that the plant will get larger than reported.) After preparing the planting beds, dig a planting hole for each rose and add half a bag of well-aged steer manure (about one cubic foot) and mix it well with the soil. I add $1/4$ cup of epsom salts for strong growth at this time as well. (Epsom salts are available in supermarkets or drugstores.) If you are planting bare-root roses, mound the soil in the hole and spread out the roots evenly over the mound. The depth at which you plant them is determined by the climate you live in. In mild-winter areas the bud union (where the upper part of the bush was grafted to the rootstock) should be right at 1 or 2 inches above the soil surface level. In cold-winter climates place the bud union 1 to 2 inches below the soil surface level. (The colder the climate, the lower the bud union.) Finish filling in the hole with soil and gently tamp it in place. Build up a small watering basin, and water the rose in well. Then comes my secret formula for success: I mulch with a 2-inch layer of alfalfa meal or alfalfa pellets, mixed or topped off with 2 to 3 inches of an organic mulch, such as compost. Alfalfa meal or pellets slowly add nitrogen and trace elements to the soil. (I buy my alfalfa meal, or the pellets, from the local feedstore. The pellets are sold as rabbit food.) Keep all mulch at least six inches away from the base of the rose. Drip irrigation is the best possible method of keeping roses watered, as it keeps the foliage dry, a critical issue with black spot and rusts.

# appendix B
# pest and
# disease
# control

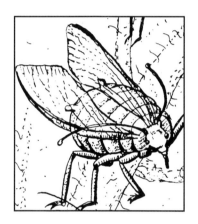

The following sections cover a large number of pests and diseases. An individual gardener, however, will encounter few such problems in a lifetime of gardening. Good garden planning, good hygiene, and an awareness of major symptoms will keep problems to a minimum and give you many hours to enjoy your garden.

While some edible flowers are as tasty to garden pests as they are to us, many edible flowers are herbs and have far fewer pests than the standard vegetable or flower garden. Deer and rabbits, say, are seldom interested in most herbs. Pest insects as well are seldom drawn to herbs, but in many cases beneficial insects are. Plants such as cilantro, dill, thyme, and fennel all produce many small flowers that provide nectar crucial to many beneficial insects at different stages of their life. Further, many flowering herbs like anise hyssop, chives, rosemary, sage, borage, chamomile, fennel, and lavender not only give us edible flowers but provide nectar and pollen to both domestic and wild bees. When you are aware of the insect world around you, you can help maintain the balance in your garden, and so benefit not only your plants, but all the plants in your neighborhood.

In a nutshell, few insects are potential problems; most are either neutral or beneficial to the garden. Given the chance, the beneficials do much of your insect control for you, provided that you don't use pesticides, as pesticides are apt to kill the beneficial insects as well as the problem insects. Like predatory lions stalking zebra, predatory ladybugs (lady beetles) or lacewing larvae hunt and eat aphids that might be attracted to your roses, say. Or a miniwasp parasitoid will lay eggs in the aphids. If you spray those aphids, even with a so-called benign pesticide such as insecticidal soap or pyrethrum, you'll kill off the ladybugs, lacewings, and that baby parasitoid wasp too. Most insecticides are broad spectrum, which means that they kill insects indiscriminately, not just the pests. In my opinion, organic gardeners who regularly use organic broad-spectrum insecticides have missed this point. If you use an "organic" pesticide, you may actually be eliminating a truly organic means of control, the beneficial insects.

Unfortunately, many gardeners are not aware of the benefits of the predator-prey

relationship and are not able to recognize beneficial insects. The following sections will help you identify both helpful and pest organisms. A more detailed aid for identifying insects is *Rodale's Color Handbook of Garden Insects*, by Anna Carr. A hand lens is an invaluable and inexpensive tool that will also help you identify the insects in your garden.

## Predators and Parasitoids

Insects that feed on other insects are divided into two types, the predators and the parasitoids. Predators are mobile. They stalk plants looking for such plant feeders as aphids and mites. Parasitoids, on the other hand, are insects that develop in or on the bodies, pupae, or eggs of other host insects. Most parasitoids are minute wasps or flies whose larvae (young stages) eat other insects from within. Some of these wasps are so small, they can develop within an aphid or an insect egg. Or one parasitoid egg can divide into several identical cells, each developing into identical miniwasp larvae, which can then kill an entire caterpillar. Though nearly invisible to most gardeners, parasitoids are the most specific and effective means of insect control.

The predator-prey relationship can be a fairly stable situation; when the natural system is working properly, pest insects inhabiting the garden along with the predators and parasites seldom become a problem. Sometimes, though, the system breaks down. For example, a number of imported pests have taken hold in this country. Unfortunately, when such organisms were brought here, their natural predators did not accompany them. Two pesky examples are the European brown snail and Japanese beetles. Neither organism has natural enemies in this country that provide sufficient controls. Where they occur, it is sometimes necessary to use physical means or selective pesticides that kill only the problem insect. Weather extremes sometime produce imbalances as well. For example, long stretches of hot, dry weather favor grasshoppers that eat gardens because the diseases that keep these insects in check are more prevalent under moist conditions.

There are other situations in which the predator-prey relationship gets out of balance because many gardening practices inadvertently work in favor of the pests. For example, when gardeners spray with broad-spectrum pesticides regularly, not all the insects in the garden are killed—and since predators and parasitoids generally reproduce more slowly than do the pests, regular spraying usually tips the balance in favor of the pests. Further, all too often the average yard has few plants that produce nectar for beneficial insects; instead, it is filled with grass and shrubs so that when a few tastier plants are put in, they attract the pests. Not only will the practices outlined here help you create a garden free of most pest problems, but, with the right plants, you can probably help eliminate other pest problems you or your neighbors have struggled with for years.

## Attracting Beneficial Insects

Besides reducing your use of pesticides, the key to keeping a healthy balance in your garden is providing a diversity of plants, including plenty of nectar- and pollen-producing plants. Nectar is the primary food of the adult stage, and some larval stages, of many beneficial insects. The small flowers on the many herbs are just what tiny beneficial insects need. Many composites (flowers in the *Asteraceae* family), such as calendulas and the single-petaled chrysanthemums, also offer abundant nectar because their centers contain numerous tiny flowers, each a source of nectar.

Following are a few of the predatory and parasitoid insects that are helpful in the garden. Their preservation and protection should be a major goal of your pest control strategy.

**Ground beetles** and their larvae are all predators. Most adult ground beetles are fairly large black beetles that scurry out from under lavender or other perennials when you disturb them. Their favorite foods are soft-bodied larvae like root maggots; some even eat snails and slugs. If supplied with an undisturbed place to live, like your compost area or groupings of perennial plantings, ground beetles will be long-lived residents of your garden.

**Lacewings** are one of the most effective insect predators in the home garden. They are small, green or brown gossamer-winged insects that in their adult stage eat flower nectar, pollen, aphid honeydew, and sometimes aphids and mealybugs. In the larval stage they look like little tan alligators. Called aphid lions, the larvae are fierce predators of aphids, mealybugs, mites, thrips, and whiteflies.

**Lady Beetles (ladybugs)** are the best known of the beneficial garden insects. Actually, there are about four hundred species of lady beetles in North America alone. They come in a variety of colors and markings in addition to the familiar red with black spots, but they are never green. Lady beetles and their fierce-looking alligator-shaped larvae eat aphids, mealybugs, and other small insects.

**Spiders** are close relatives of insects. There are hundreds of species, and they are some of the most effective controllers of pest insects.

**Syrphid flies** (also called flowerflies or hover flies) look like small bees hovering over flowers, but they have only two wings. Most have yellow and black stripes on their body. Their larvae are small green maggots that live on leaves, eating aphids, mealybugs, other small insects, and mites.

**Wasps** are a large family of insects with transparent wings. Unfortunately, the few large wasps that sting have given wasps a bad name. In fact, all wasps are either insect predators or parasitoids. The parasitoid adult female lays her eggs in such insects as aphids and caterpillars, and the developing larvae devour the host.

## Pests

The following pests are sometimes a problem in the garden.

**Aphids** are soft-bodied, small, green, black, pink, gold, or gray insects that produce many generations in one season. They suck plant juices and exude honeydew.

Sometimes leaves under the aphids turn black from a secondary mold growing on the nutrient-rich how. Aphids are primarily a problem on roses, broccoli, and chives. A buildup of aphids can indicate the plant is under stress—are your roses getting enough water, or sunlight, say? Check first to see if stress is a problem and then try to correct it. If there is a large infestation, look for aphid mummies and other natural enemies mentioned above. Mummies are swollen brown or metallic-looking aphids. Inside the mummy a wasp parasitoid is growing. They are valuable, so keep them. To remove aphids generally, wash the foliage with a strong blast of water and cut back the foliage if they persist. Fertilize and water the plant, and check on it in a few days. Repeat with the water spray a few more times. In extreme situations spray with insecticidal soap or a neem product.

A number of **beetles** are garden pests. They include cucumber and Japanese beetles.

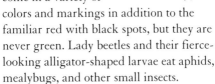

Cucumber beetles are ladybug-like green or yellow-green beetles with either black stripes or black spots. Japanese beetles are fairly large metallic blue or green with coppery wings. Cucumber beetles can be a problem on squash plants and may sometimes be found down inside the blossoms. Japanese beetles are often a problem on roses.

Beetles such as Japanese and cucumber beetles, if not in great numbers, can be controlled by hand picking—in the morning is best, when the beetles are slower. Knock them into a bowl of soapy water. Larger populations may need more control, however. Try a spray of insecticidal soap first; if you're not successful, use neem or pyrethrum. Japanese beetles were accidentally introduced into the United States early in this century and are now a serious problem in the eastern part of the country. The larval stage (a grub) lives on the roots of grasses, and the adult beetle skeletonizes the leaves of many plants and chews on flowers and buds. Certain species of beneficial nematodes have proved effective in controlling the larvae of Japanese beetles. Milky-spore, a naturally occurring soilborne disease, is also used to control the beetles in the larval stage, although the disease is slow to work.

**Nematodes** are microscopic round worms that inhabit the soil in most of the United States, particularly in the Southeast. Most nematode species live on decaying matter or are predatory on other nematodes, insects, algae, or bacteria. (See the following section on "Beneficial Nematodes".) A few types are parasitic, attaching themselves to the roots of perennials, including daylilies, lavender, and rosemary. The symptoms of nematode damage are stunted-looking plants and small swellings or lesions on the roots.

To control nematodes, keep your soil high in organic matter (to encourage fungi and predatory nematodes, both of which act as biological controls). Some success has been recorded by interplanting with marigolds, which seem to inhibit the nematodes, and by using applications of beneficial nematodes available from insectaries. If all else fails, grow the susceptible plants in containers with sterilized soil.

**Snails and slugs** are not insects, of course, but mollusks. Marigolds, violets, calendulas, and pansies are among the plants they relish. They feed at night and can go dormant for months in times of drought or low food supply. In the absence of effective natural enemies (a few snail eggs are consumed by predatory beetles and earwigs), several snail-control strategies can be recommended. Since snails and slugs are most active after rain or irrigation, go out and destroy them on such nights. Only repeated forays provide adequate control. Planter boxes with a strip of copper applied along the top perimeter boards keep slugs and snails out—they won't cross the barrier. Any overhanging leaves that can provide a bridge into the bed will defeat the barrier. You will get some control by putting out shallow containers filled to within an inch of the top with cheap beer. The pests crawl in and are not able to crawl out.

**Spider mites** are among the few arachnids (spiders and their kin) that pose a problem in the garden. Mites are so small that a hand lens is usually needed to see them. They become a problem when they reproduce in great numbers and suck on the leaves of plants such as marigolds, roses, rosemary, sage, strawberries, and thyme. A symptom of serious mite damage is stippling on the leaves in the form of tiny white or yellow spots, sometimes accompanied by tiny webs. The major natural predators of spider mites are predatory mites, mite-eating thrips, and syrphid flies.

Mites are most likely to thrive on dusty leaves and in dry, warm weather. A routine foliage wash and misting of sensitive plants helps control mites. Mites are seldom a serious problem unless you have used heavy-duty pesticides that kill off predatory mites or if you are growing plants in the house. Cut plants back, and if you're using heavy-duty pesticides, stop the applications, and the balance could return. Serious infestations usually are controlled by using horticultural oil. For plants in the house, cut back foliage, wash it well, quarantine the plants, and apply refined horticultural oil.

If mites persist, discard the plants. (*Caution:* Always tend to plants with mites last, or wash tools well, as mites can hitchhike on tools to other plants.)

## Pest Control

**Beneficial Nematodes (Entomopathogenic Nematodes)** are microscopic round worms. Many nematodes are selective predators of certain insects, especially soil-dwelling insects. They can be purchased for use on various pests, including Japanese beetle and cucumber beetle larvae. Most beneficial nematodes must be mixed with water and need warm weather to survive. Be sure you are using the species for the pest you have and read the directions carefully for application. Since they are selective, they do not harm earthworms or other organisms.

**Insecticidal soap sprays** are effective against many pest insects, including caterpillars, aphids, mites, and whiteflies. They can be purchased or you can make a soap spray at home. As a rule, I recommend purchasing insecticidal soap, such as the one made by Safer Corporation, as it has been carefully formulated to give the most effective control with the least risk to your plants. If you do make your own, use a liquid dishwashing soap; do not use caustic or germicidal soaps.

**Horticultural oils** have been used for many years as dormant sprays on fruit trees. Today most horticultural oils are lightweight summer or "superior" horticultural oils that have been refined to remove the compounds that damage the leaves of growing plants. The more refined oil can be used on some plants to control pest insects and diseases; however, they do smother beneficial insects as well as pests. Follow the directions for summer concentrations. Always test the oil on a small part of the plant first, as some plants are very sensitive to oil sprays and will burn or lose their leaves. In addition, don't use horticultural oil on very hot days or on plants that are moisture-stressed.

**Neem**-oil extracts, which are derived from the neem tree (*Azadirachta indica*), have relatively low toxicity to mammals but are effective against a wide range of insects, including different types of aphids, cucumber beetles, and spider mites. They work in a variety of different ways. Check the label for more information. Neem is still fairly new in use in the United States. Although neem was thought at first to be harmless to beneficial insects, studies now show that some parasitoid beneficial insects that feed on neem-treated pest insects were unable to survive to adulthood.

**Pyrethrum,** a botanical insecticide, is toxic to a wide range of insects but has relatively low toxicity to most mammals and breaks down quickly in the presence of sunlight. The active ingredients in pyrethrum are pyrethins derived from chrysanthemum flowers. Do not confuse pyrethrum with pyrethoids which are much more toxic synthetics that do not biodegrade as quickly. Many pyrethrums have a synergist, piperonyl butoxide (PBO), added to increase the effectiveness. However, there is evidence that PBO may affect the human nervous system. Try to use pyrethrums without PBO added. Wear gloves, goggles, and a respirator when using pyrethrum.

## Diseases

Plant diseases are potentially far more damaging to your plants than are most insects. Diseases are also more difficult to control because they usually grow inside the plant, and plants do not respond with immune mechanisms comparable to those that protect animals. Consequently, most plant-disease-control strategies feature prevention rather than control. Hence, the constant admonition to plant in soil with good drainage.

To keep diseases under control, it is very important to plant the "right plant in the right place." For instance, many perennials, such as lavender or sage, prefer a dry environment and will often develop root rot in soil that is continually wet. Check the cultural needs of a plant before placing it in your garden. Proper light, exposure, temperature, fertilization, and moisture are important factors in disease control. Diseased plants should always be discarded,

not composted. The entries for individual plants in the "Encyclopedia of Edible Flowers" (page 29) give specific cultural information.

**Damping off** is caused by a parasitic fungus that lives near the soil surface and attacks new young plants in their early seedling stage. It causes them to wilt and fall over just where they emerge from the soil. This fungus thrives under dark, humid conditions, so it can often be thwarted by keeping the seedlings in a bright, well-ventilated place in fast-draining soil.

**Powdery mildew** affects many plants, including roses, bee balm, lilacs, peas, and squash. This fungus disease appears as a powdery white growth on the leaves and causes new leaves and stem tips to curl. Whenever possible, plant resistant varieties. Make sure the plant has good air circulation, full sun, and adequate water. Powdery mildew is encouraged by fine films of water, such as from fog or high humidity, and discouraged by heavy flows of water. In some cases, it can be washed off with water from a hose; do so early in the day so the foliage will dry quickly. Spraying with refined horticultural oil, liquid sulfur, or baking soda every few weeks also controls mildew. (For baking soda spray, use 1 teaspoon baking soda to 1 quart warm water, with 1 teaspoon insecticidal soap to help the solution stick.) Test on a small part of the plant first. With some plants, such as peas and squashes, powdery mildew worsens toward the end of the season; it is best to just go ahead and remove the plant. Thoroughly clean up garden debris to help eliminate overwintering spores.

**Root rot** and **crown rot** are common problems for many perennials. A number of different fungi cause these rots; they are usually brought on by poor drainage, overwatering, or the crown (base) of the plant being covered by soil, mulch, or debris. The classic symptom of root rot is wilting—even after a rain or when a plant is well watered. Sometimes the wilting starts with only a few branches; other times the whole plant wilts. Plants are often stunted and yellow as well. The diagnosis is complete when the dead plant is pulled up to reveal rotten, black roots. There is no cure

for root and crown rots once they involve the whole plant. Remove and destroy the plant and correct the drainage problem.

**Rust** and **black spot** are fungal diseases that affect roses. Rust appears as orange spots on the underside of leaves. Black spot manifests as dark spots on leaves and canes; it can completely defoliate a plant. Plant resistant varieties if these diseases are prevalent in your area. Make sure the plant has good air circulation, full sun, and adequate water. Do not overhead water. Prune infected leaves and destroy them. Plants will usually recover. But in some cases, such as in cool, humid climates where black spot is prevalent, letting the plant defoliate often seriously weakens the plant. Spraying with refined horticultural oil, liquid sulfur, or baking soda is an effective control. Spray as directed previously in "Powdery Mildew," and repeat every seven to fourteen days while the problems persist.

# herb resources

## Sources for Seeds and Plants

Chiltern Seeds
Bortree Stile
Ulverston, Cumbria
LA 12 7PB, England
*Large variety of seeds, including herbs and Oriental greens*

The Cook's Garden
P. O. Box 535
Londonderry, VT 05148
*Superior varieties of vegetables and herbs*

Evergreen Y. H. Enterprises
P. O. Box 17538
Anaheim, CA 92817
Catalog: $2.00 U.S.; $2.50 in Canada
*Oriental vegetables and herbs*

Fox Hollow Seed Company
P. O. Box 148
McGrann, PA 16236
Catalog: $1.00
*Herbs, vegetables, flowers, heirlooms*

The Gourmet Gardener
8650 College Boulevard
Overland Park, KS 66210
*Herbs, vegetables, edible flowers, seeds*

Le Jardin du Gourmet
P. O. Box 75
St. Johnsbury Center, VT 05863-0075
*Herb plants and seeds*

Johnny's Selected Seeds
Foss Hill Road
Albion, ME 04910-9731
*Excellent selection of herb and vegetable seeds; unusual varieties*

Logee's Greenhouses
141 North Street
Danielson, CT 06239
Catalog: $3.00
*Herb plants and seeds, ornamental perennial plants, many unusual and tender varieties*

Native Seeds/SEARCH
526 North Fourth Avenue
Tucson, AZ 85705
Membership: $20.00
Low income/student: $12.00
Catalog: $1.00
*Nonprofit organization working to preserve Southwestern Native American seeds; membership includes 10 percent discount on catalog items; unusual Southwestern and Mexican herbs and vegetables*

Nichols Garden Nursery
1190 North Pacific Highway NE
Albany, OR 97321-4580
*Seeds and plants of herbs, flowers, vegetables; many unusual varieties*

Redwood City Seed Company
P. O. Box 361
Redwood City, CA 94064
Catalog: $1.00
*Herb and vegetable seeds; many chili pepper seeds and unusual varieties*

Renee's Garden
Look for seed racks in better retail nurseries. For more information call toll-free (888) 880-7228 or look for her on-line at garden.com/reneesgarden.

Richters
357 Highway 47
Goodwood, Ontario
Canada L0C 1A0
*Most extensive selection of herb seeds and plants available in North America*

Seeds of Change
P. O. Box 15700
Sante Fe, NM 87506-5700
*Organically grown vegetable and herb seeds*

Shepherd's Garden Seeds
30 Irene Street
Torrington, CT 06790
*Quality varieties of vegetable, herb, and flower seeds and plants*

Well-Sweep Herb Farm
205 Mt. Bethel Road
Port Murray, NJ 07865
Catalog: $2.00
*No shipments to California; extensive selection of common and uncommon herb seeds, plants, and dried herbs*

## Seed Exchanges

Flower and Herb Exchange
3076 North Winn Road
Decorah, IA 52101
Membership fee: $10.00
*Nonprofit organization dedicated to saving diversity; rare and heirloom flower and herb seeds*

## Gardening and Cooking Suppliers

Balducci's
Mail Order Division
334 East Eleventh Street
New York, NY 10003
*Food products, fancy herbs and seasonings*

Chef's Catalog
3215 Commercial Avenue
Northbrook, IL 60062
*Professional and home cooking supplies*

Dean and DeLuca
Mail Order Division
110 Greene Street
Suite 304
New York, NY 10012
*Food products, fancy herbs and oils, cooking equipment*

Gardener's Supply Company
128 Intervale Road
Burlington, VT 05401
*Gardening tools and supplies*

The Natural Gardening Company
217 San Anselmo Avenue
San Anselmo, CA 94960

Peaceful Valley Farm Supply
P. O. Box 2209
Grass Valley, CA 95945
*Gardening supplies, organic fertilizers*

Penzeys, Ltd.
P.O. Box 1448
Waukesha, WI 53187
*Specializes in dried herbs and spices*

Sur La Table
Catalog Division
1765 Sixth Avenue South
Seattle, WA 98134
*Cooking equipment*

Williams-Sonoma
Mail Order Department
P.O. Box 7456
San Francisco, CA 94120-7456
*Cooking equipment*

# Books and Publications

American Horticulture Society. The Heat Map. 1-800-777-7931, Extension 45. Cost: $15.00.

Barash, Cathy Wilkinson. *Edible Flowers: From Garden to Palate.* Golden, Colo.: Fulcrum Publishing, 1993.

The editors of Sunset magazines and Sunset books. *Sunset National Garden Book.* Menlo Park, Calif.: Sunset Publishing Co., 1997.

———. *Sunset Western Garden Book.* Menlo Park, Calif.: Sunset Publishing Co., 1995.

Gilkeson, Linda, Pam Pierce, and Miranda Smith. *Rodale's Pest and Disease Problem Solver: A Chemical-Free Guide to Keeping Your Garden Healthy.* Emmaus, Pa.: Rodale Press, 1996.

Hill, Madalene, and Gwen Barclay, with Jean Hardy. *Southern Herb Growing.* Fredericksburg, Tex.: Shearer Publishing, 1987.

Hopkinson, Patricia, Diane Miske, Jerry Parsons, and Holly Shimizu. *Herb Gardening* (American Garden Guides). New York: Pantheon Books, 1994.

Kowalchik, Claire, and William H. Hylton, ed. *Rodale's Illustrated Encyclopedia of Herbs.* Emmaus, Pa.: Rodale Press, 1987.

Lathrop, Norma Jean. *Herbs: How to Select, Grow and Enjoy.* Tucson: H. P. Books, 1981.

Olkowski, William, Sheila Daar, and Helga Olkowski. *The Gardener's Guide to Common Sense Pest Control.* Newtown, Conn.: Taunton Press, 1995.

Saville, Carole. *Exotic Herbs.* New York: Henry Holt and Co., 1997.

Shepherd, Renee. *Recipes from a Kitchen Garden.* Felton, Calif.: Shepherd's Garden Publishing, 1987.

Shepherd, Renee and Fran Raboff. *Recipes from a Kitchen Garden,* Volume II. Felton, Calif. Shepherd, Renee, Shepherd's Garden Publishing, 1991.

Whealy, Diane. *1997 Flower and Herb Exchange.* Decorah, Iowa: Seed Saver Publications, 1997. To order, contact the Flower and Herb Exchange, 3076 North Winn Road, Decorah, IA 52101. Membership fee (includes book): $10.00.

Wilson, Jim. *Landscaping with Herbs.* Boston: Houghton Mifflin, 1994. *Gardening supplies, organic fertilizers, beneficial nematodes*

# flower resources

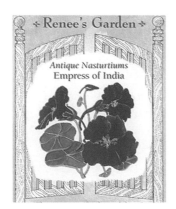

Renee's Garden
Antique Nasturtiums
Empress of India

## Sources for Seeds and Plants

The Antique Rose Emporium
9300 Lueckemeyer Road
Brenam, TX 77833-6453
Catalog: $5.00
*Great selection of old rose culti-vars, species, and disease-resistant roses*

Chiltern Seeds
Bortree Stile
Ulverston, Cumbria
LA 12 7PB, England
*Large variety of vegetable and flower seeds*

The Cook's Garden
P.O. Box 535
Londonderry, VT 05148
*Superior varieties of vegetables, herbs, and flowers*

Evergreen Y. H. Enterprises
P.O. Box 17538
Anaheim, CA 92817
Catalog: $2.00 U.S.; $2.50 in Canada
*Oriental vegetables and herbs*

Flower and Herb Exchange
3076 North Winn Road
Decorah, IA 52101
Membership fee: $10.00
*Heirloom flower and herb seeds*

Fox Hollow Seed Company
P.O. Box 148
McGrann, PA 16236
Catalog: $1.00
*Herbs, vegetables, flowers, and heirlooms*

The Gourmet Gardener
8650 College Boulevard
Overland Park, KS 66210
*Herbs, vegetables, and edible flower seeds*

Johnny's Selected Seeds
Foss Hill Road
Albion, ME 04910-9731
*Excellent selection of herb, vegetable, and flower seeds*

Harris Seeds and Nursery

P.O. Box 22960
Rochester, NY 14692-2960
*Vegetable, herb, and flower seeds*

J. L. Hudson, Seedsman
Star Route 2, Box 337
La Honda, CA 94020
For catalog: P.O. Box 1058,
Redwood City, CA 94064
Catalog: $1.00
*Specializes in seeds of a huge variety of flowers and vegetables*

Logee's Greenhouses
141 North Street
Danielson, CT 06239
Catalog: $3.00
*Herb plants and seeds, ornamen-tal perennial plants, and citrus; many unusual varieties*

Niche Gardens
1111 Dawson Road
Chapel Hill, NC 27516
*Wildflowers and perennial plants*

Nichols Garden Nursery
1190 North Pacific Highway NE
Albany, OR 97321-4580
*Seeds and plants of herbs, flowers, and vegetables; unusual varieties*

Pinetree Garden Seeds
Box 300
New Gloucester, ME 04260
*Good selection of herbs, flowers, and vegetables*

Renee's Garden
*Look for seed racks in better retail nurseries. For more information call toll-free (888) 880-7228 or look for her on-line at garden.com/reneesgarden.*

Richters Herb Catalogue
357 Highway 47
Goodwood, Ontario
L0C 1A0 Canada
*Most extensive selection of herb seeds and plants available to North America*

Seeds Blüm
HC 33 Box 2057
Boise, ID 83706
Catalog: $3.00; first-class option: $5.00
*Open-pollinated vegetables, herbs, and heirloom edible flowers.*

Seeds of Change
P.O. Box 15700
Sante Fe, NM 87506-5700
*Organically grown vegetable, herb, and flower seeds*

Seed Savers Exchange
3076 North Winn Road
Decorah, IA 52101
Membership fee: $25.00
Low-income/senior/student: $20.00; In Canada: $30.00
Overseas: $40.00
*Vegetable and fruit seeds. Catalog for purchasing selected seeds is free to nonmembers and members.*

Select Seeds Antique Flowers
180 Stickney Road
Union, CT 06076-4617
Catalog: $1.00
*Specializes in species and antique flower seeds*

Shepherd's Garden Seeds
30 Irene Street
Torrington, CT 06790
*Quality varieties of vegetable, herb, and flower seeds and plants*

Sonoma Antique Apple Nursery
4395 Westside Road
Healdsburg, CA 95448
*Good selection of antique apples and other fruit trees*

Stokes Seeds, Inc.
P.O. Box 548
Buffalo, NY 14240
*Vegetables and flower seeds; large sel-ection of annual edible flower seeds*

Territorial Seed Company
P.O. Box 157
Cottage Grove, OR 97424-0061
*Good selection of vegetable, herb, and flower seeds*

Wayside Gardens

1 Garden Lane
Hodges, SC 29695
*Plants of ornamental perennials
and shrubs*

Well-Sweep Herb Farm
205 Mt. Bethel Road
Port Murray, NJ 07865
Catalog: $2.00
No shipment to California.
*Extensive selection of herb seeds,
plants, and dried herbs*

White Flower Farm
P.O. Box 50
Litchfield, CT 06759
*Carries a wide range ornamental
plants and a selection of disease-
resistant roses*

## Organizations

American Horticulture Society
7931 East Boulevard Drive
Alexandria, VA 22308
*To purchase* The Heat Map, *call
1-800-777-7931, Extension 45.
Cost: $15.00*

The American Rose Society
P.O. Box 30000
Shreveport, LA 71130
1-800-637-6534
*Definitely worth joining, as it can
direct you to rose experts in your
area who are knowledgeable
about rose varieties and care for
your climate*

The Canadian Rose Society
10 Fairfax Crescent
Scarborough, Ontario
M1L 1Z8 Canada

Flower and Herb Exchange
3076 North Winn Road
Decorah, IA 52101
Membership fee: $10.00
*Nonprofit organization dedicated
to saving diversity. Members join
an extensive network of gardeners
who save and exchange flower
and herb seeds*

The Royal National Rose
Society
Chiswell Green
St. Albans, Hertfordshire
AL2 3NR England

Seed Savers Exchange
3076 North Winn Road
Decorah, IA 52101
Membership fee: $25.00
Low-income/senior/student:
$20.00
In Canada: $30.00  Overseas:
$40.00
*Nonprofit organization dedicated
to saving diversity. Members join
an extensive network of gardeners
who save and exchange vegetable
and fruit seeds*

## Bibliography

Barash, Cathy Wilkinson.
*Edible Flowers from
Garden to Palate.* Golden,
Colo.: Fulcrum
Publishing, 1993.

Brown, Deni. *Encyclopedia of
Herbs and Their Uses.*
London: Dorling
Kindersley, 1995.

Bryan, John E., and Coralie
Castle. *The Edible
Ornamental Garden.* San
Francisco: 101
Productions, 1974.

Bubel, Nancy. *The New Seed-
Starter's Handbook.*
Emmaus, Pa.: Rodale
Press, 1988.

Carr, Anna. *Rodale's Color
Handbook of Garden
Insects.* Emmaus, Pa.:
Rodale Press, 1979.

Cathey, Dr. H. R. Marc. *Heat-
Zone Gardening: How to
Choose Plants That Thrive
in Your Region's Warmest
Weather.* Alexandria, Va.:
Time-Life Custom

Publishing, 1998.

Creasy, Rosalind. *The Complete
Book of Edible Land-
scaping.* San Francisco:
Sierra Club Books, 1982.

Druitt, Liz, and Michael Shoup.
*Landscaping with Antique
Roses.* Newtown, Conn.:
Taunton Press, 1992.

Editors of Sunset Books and
Sunset Magazine. *Sunset
National Garden Book.*
Menlo Park, Calif.:
Sunset Books, 1997.

Foster, Steven, and James A.
Duke. *A Field Guide to
Medicinal Plants —
Eastern and Central North
America.* Boston:
Houghton Mifflin, 1990.

Gilkeson, Linda, Pam Peirce,
and Miranda Smith.
*Rodale's Pest and Disease
Problem Solver: A
Chemical-Free Guide to
Keeping Your Garden
Healthy.* Emmaus, Pa.:
Rodale Press, 1996.

Hedrick, U. P., ed. *Sturtevant's
Edible Plants of the World.*
Reprint. New York:
Dover Publications, 1972.

Hill, Madalene, and Gwen
Barclay with Jean Hardy.
*Southern Herb Growing.*
Fredericksburg, Tex.:
Shearer Publishing, 1987.

Hopkinson, Patricia, and Diane
Miske, Jerry Parsons,
Holly Shimizu. *The
American Garden Guides:
Herb Gardening.* New
York: Pantheon Books,
1994.

Kowalchik, Claire, and
William H. Hylton, ed.
*Rodale's Illustrated
Encyclopedia of Herbs.*

Emmaus, Pa.: Rodale
Press, 1987.

Lampe, Dr. Kenneth F., and
Mary Ann McCann.
*AMA Handbook of
Poisonous and Injurious
Plants.* Chicago:
American Medical
Association of Chicago,
1985.

Larkcom, Joy. *The Salad
Garden.* New York:
Viking, 1984.

McKeon, Judith C. *The
Encyclopedia of Roses: An
Organic Guide to Growing
and Enjoying America's
Favorite Flower.*
Emmaus, Pa.: Rodale
Press, 1995.

Ogden, Shepherd. *Step by Step
Organic Flower
Gardening.* New York:
HarperCollins
Publishers, 1995.

——. *Step by Step Organic
Vegetable Gardening: The
Gardening Classic Revised
and Updated.* New York:
HarperCollins
Publishers, 1992.

Olkowski, William, Sheila
Daar, and Helga
Olkowski. *The Gardener's
Guide to Common Sense
Pest Control.* Newtown,
Conn.: Taunton Press,
1995.

Oster, Maggie. *Flowering Herbs.*
Stanford, Conn.:
Longmeadow Press,
1991.

——. *The Rose Book: How to
Grow Roses Organically
and Use Them in Over 50
Beautiful Crafts.*
Emmaus, Pa.: Rodale
Press, 1994.

Peterson, Lee Allen, and Roger Tory Peterson. *Field Guide to Edible Wild Plants: Eastern and Central North America.* Boston: Houghton Mifflin, 1982.

Philips, Roger. *Wild Food.* Boston: Little, Brown, 1986.

Proctor, Rob. *Annuals: Yearly Classics for the Contemporary Garden.* New York: HarperCollins Publishers, 1991.

Reilly, Ann. *Park's Success with Seeds.* Greenwood, S. C.: Geo. W. Park Seed Co., 1978.

Saville, Carole. *Exotic Herbs.* New York: Henry Holt and Co., 1997.

Schneider, Elizabeth. *Uncommon Fruits and Vegetables: A Commonsense Guide.* New York: Harper & Row, 1986.

Shepherd, Renee. *Recipes from a Kitchen Garden.* Felton, Calif.: Shepherd's Garden Publishing, 1987.

Smittle, Delilah, ed. *Rodale's Complete Garden Problem Solver.* Emmaus, Pa.: Rodale Press, 1997.

Walheim, Lance. *The Natural Rose Gardener.* Tucson, Ariz.: Ironwood Press, 1994.

Whealy, Diane. *1997 Flower and Herb Exchange.* Decorah, Iowa: Seed Saver Publications, 1997.

# acknowledgments

My garden is the foundation for my books, photography, and recipes. For nearly twelve months of the year we toil to keep it beautiful and bountiful. Unlike most gardens, as it is a photo studio and trial plot, it must look glorious, be healthy, and produce for the kitchen. To complicate the maintenance, all the beds are changed at least twice a year. Needless to say it is a large undertaking. For two decades a quartet of talented organic gardener/cooks have not only given it hundreds of hours of loving attention, but they have also been generous with their vast knowledge of plants. Together we have forged our concept of gardening and cooking, much of which I share with you in this series of garden cookbooks.

I wish to thank Wendy Krupnick for giving the garden such a strong foundation and Joe Queirolo for maintaining it for many years and lending it such a gentle and sure hand. For the last decade Jody Main and Duncan Minalga have helped me expand my garden horizons. No matter how complex the project they enthusiastically rise to the occasion. In the kitchen, I am most for-tunate to have Gudi Riter, a very talented cook who developed many of her skills in Germany and France. I thank her for the help she provides as we create recipes and present them in all their glory.

I want to thank Carole Saville who has generously shared her vast knowledge of herbs and given me a firm footing. Over the years we have collaborated on magazine columns and books, and much of her talent appears in these pages. Herbs have different requirements, depending on the climate in which they are grown. I depend on herb mavens; Rose Marie Nichols McGee of Nichols Garden Nursery in Oregon, Jim Wilson in South Carolina, Madeline Hill and Gwen Barkley in Texas, Louise Hyde at Well-Sweep Herb Farm in New Jersey, Lucinda Hutson in Texas, and Ron Zimmerman in Washington for their expertise, and I thank them for shar-ing their gardens.

I thank Dayna Lane for her steady hand and editorial assistance. In addition to day-to-day compilations, she joins me on our constant search for the most effective organic pest controls, superior herb varieties, and the best sources for plants.

I would also like to thank a large supporting cast: my husband Robert who gives such quality technical advice and loving support; my daughter-in-law Julie Creasy, who is always available for recipe testing or a photo shoot; Nancy Favier for her occasional help in the garden and office; Jesse Cool, owner of Flea Street Café in California, for her wonderful recipes; Renee Shepherd of Renee's Garden, and Cathy Barash, editor of Meredith Books, for sharing her information and enthusiasm; Jane Whitfield, Linda Gunnarson, and David Humphrey, who were integral to the initial vision of this book; Kathryn Sky-Peck for providing the style and quality of the layout, and Marcie Hawthorne for the lovely drawings. Heartfelt thanks to Eric Oey and to the entire Periplus staff, especially Deane Norton and Sonia MacNeil, for their help. Finally, I would like to thank my editor, Isabelle Bleecker, for her gentle guidance, attention to detail, and thoughtful presence.